'with all faults'

'mea culpa'

David Low

Holywell Street, 'Booksellers' Row', London, 1898, wash drawing by Hanslip Fletcher

DAVID LOW

'with all faults'

INTRODUCTION BY
GRAHAM GREENE

TEHRAN
THE AMATE PRESS
1973

THE AMATE PRESS, TEHRAN
Distributed by
DAVID LOW BOOKSELLERS LTD
Emmington, Chinnor, Oxford

Designed by Bernard Crossland
PRINTED IN GREAT BRITAIN
BY BURGESS AND SON (ABINGDON) LTD
ABINGDON, BERKS.

To my bookseller friends
and my partners
Billy Howard and
Robin Waterfield

CONTENTS

LIST OF PLATES

PREFACE

When in 1926 I became a cataloguer at Hodgson's the book auctioneers in Chancery Lane, I soon learned the use of the letters 'w.a.f.'. They were placed after the description of a book in which there were probably imperfections, and stood for the words 'with all faults'.

Such auctioneers' lots were avoided by the perfectionist, but for me they held intrigue. I was for these waifs and their buyers. After a lifetime of bookselling I am still for them both, indeed become so much part of their world that *with all faults* seemed a natural title for a book about our 'dusty idiosyncratic world'.

If the Amate Press, Tehran, seems rather a long way out, its imprint was quite as natural a choice as was that of the title. My old partner, Robin Waterfield, had left me in 1950 to work with the Church Missionary Society in Persia, but not even a missionary can forget the happier tricks of his former life. Last summer when Robin wrote me about his latest bibliographical distraction, the Amate Press, I offered him *with all faults* as his first title, and he was delighted.

To Robin I am further grateful for his patient and persistent blowing when there was little wind in his author's sail; to Ben Weinreb for his heartening welcome when port was almost made, and to Leslie Shepard for navigational corrections.

I thank Leslie Wesson for his photographs of Emmington, and Helmut Gernsheim for his of Cecil Court, also the *Oxford Mail* and fellow booksellers who helped with their own; Nicolas Bentley for his two bibliopolic drawings, and finally Bernard Crossland for the typographical distinction he has given to the book, already blessed with the Introduction by my old friend Graham Greene.

DAVID LOW

INTRODUCTION

I don't know how Freud would have interpreted them, but for more than thirty years my happiest dreams have been of second-hand bookshops: shops previously unknown to me or old familiar shops which I am revisiting. It is the familiar shops which have certainly never existed; I have come reluctantly to that conclusion. Somewhere not far from the Gare du Nord in Paris I have vivid memories of a shop at the end of a long street running uphill, a deep shop with high shelves (I had to use a ladder to reach the top of them). On at least two occasions I hunted through the shelves (there I thought I bought Apollinaire's translation of *Fanny Hill*), but when the war was over I searched for the shop in vain. Of course the shop could have disappeared, but the street itself was not there. Then there was a shop in London which occurred very frequently in my dreams; I can remember clearly its façade but not its interior. It stood somewhere in the region behind Charlotte Street before you come to the Euston Road, I never went inside, and I am sure now that there never was such a shop. I would always wake from such dreams with a sense of happiness and expectation.

At various periods of my life I have kept a diary of my dreams, and my diary for this year (1972) contains in the first seven months six dreams of secondhand bookshops. Curiously enough, for the first time, they are not happy dreams; perhaps because a loved companion with whom I used to hunt books and with whom I began to form, just after the war, a collection of Victorian detective stories died at the end of 1971. So in this year's dreams an old railway book which I am planning to give to my friend John Sutro for Christmas (he had founded the Railway Club at Oxford), when I draw it from the shelf, has lost half its cover: even the old red Nelson sevenpennies (so unaccountably maligned by George Orwell, but which I love to possess when the first editions are too expensive) prove to be all mutilated copies. Nothing in all these dreams seems good enough to buy.

My friend David Low's recollections as a bookseller have set my thoughts rambling, not only through dreams but through the small adventures and friendships of fifty years of book-hunting. (At 17 I became a wanderer in Charing Cross Road which alas! now I seldom bother to visit.)

Secondhand booksellers are among the most friendly and the most eccentric of all the characters I have known. If I had not been a writer, theirs would have been the profession I would most happily have chosen. There is the musty smell of books, and there is the sense of the treasure-hunt. For this reason I prefer the badly organized bookshop where Topography is mixed up with Astronomy and Theology with Geology and stacks of unidentified books litter the staircase to a room marked Travel, which may well contain some of my favourite Conan Doyles, *The Lost World* or *The Tragedy of the Korosko*. I am frightened of entering Maggs or Quaritch because I know there will be no personal discovery to make there, no mistake on the part of the bookseller. From David Low's recollections I realize how wrong I was to be afraid of Bain's in William IV Street. It is too late to remedy that now.

To enter properly this magic world of chance and adventure one has to be either a collector or a bookseller. I would have preferred to be a bookseller, but the opportunity escaped me in the war. During the blitz I happened to be a part-time warden attached to the same post as David Low (whom I already knew well) and little Cole, who was in those days a book 'runner'. My first patrol with Cole was in search of a parachute bomb which was said to have become entangled in the trees of one of the Bloomsbury squares. We never found it, rather to our relief. Cole took me once to see his room: I remember the shabby books stacked everywhere, even under the bed, and we agreed that one day, if we both survived the war, we would set up business together. I went off to West Africa on a different job and we lost touch. I had lost my only chance of becoming a secondhand bookseller.

To become a collector is easier. It doesn't matter what you collect, you have a key to the door. The collection is not important. It is the fun of the hunt, the characters whom you meet, the friends you make. When I was a teenager I got my first taste of collecting by buying works on Antarctic exploration; the Arctic didn't interest me. Those books have all gone. They would have a certain value now, but who cares? Before the war I collected Restoration literature because I was working on a never-published life of Rochester. They were not first editions (I couldn't afford them); they have gone too: some of them in the blitz and some I regretfully abandoned when I left England.

I am still collecting Victorian detective stories: how many I used to find in the forties at Foyle's at half-a-crown a time even though John Carter had ten years before produced his famous Scribner's catalogue which should have aroused collectors everywhere.

The value of a collection to the collector lies less in its importance, surely, than in the excitement of the hunt, and the strange places to which the hunt sometimes leads. Quite recently, with my brother Hugh, whose collection of detective stories extends from Victorian times to 1914, so that we usually hunt as a couple, I walked in pouring rain through the dismal outskirts of Leeds in a ruined area that could have been part of a Grierson documentary of the depression. The shop we sought had been included in a reliable directory, but we believed in it less and less as we got wetter and wetter between the abandoned factories. Yet when we arrived the shop *had* certainly once existed, there was a sign '. . . kseller' above a door which was no longer in place, all the windows were broken, and the floor was mysteriously littered with children's boots and shoes, good shoes too. Some meeting place of a childish Mafia? Scenes like that, and the discovery of new pubs and beers one has not previously tasted are some of the rewards of the book-hunter.

This isn't the same world as the old-established bookshop in Piccadilly, with its antiquarian section, where I went recently to pass the time, and asked if by chance they had any of the works of Wilfrid Scawen Blunt. 'What did he write, sir? Fiction?'

I think David Low is a little too kind to these expensive shops, but I suppose if one is in the trade one has to make a friendly gesture towards the well-dressed devil in his top hat and tails. The new university shops I avoid, all red brick and glass, full of secondhand academic books which were dull even when they first appeared. Alas, for Miss Dillon's shop, which survived all the bombs around Store Street, it has not the same charm today. Sometimes David Low goes too far in politeness: 'canny' is a charitable adjective to apply to the famous Mr. Wilson of Bumpus. I would have preferred 'cunning'.

No, the West End is not my hunting ground now any more than Charing Cross Road, but thank God! Cecil Court remains Cecil Court, even though David Low has moved to Oxfordshire.

From David one happy day I bought a strange eighteenth-century manuscript bound in white vellum with a handwritten title 'Hultoniana'. It cost me five guineas, a lot of money in the thirties, but I got the price back, after a little research, by writing an article in the *Spectator* on this bizarre story of a series of cruel hoaxes inflicted on an unpopular tradesman called Hulton, apparently written by one of his enemies. I have the manuscript still, 'grangerized' with an interesting letter on the eighteenth-century London shop names mentioned in it, written to me by Sir Ambrose Heal. It pleases me that in that way 'Hultoniana' cost me nothing but a little work.

Perhaps the find I value most is *The Office of the Holy Week*, translated by Walter Kirkham Blount, published in 1687 with seven engravings of Hollar and bound in tooled contemporary red morocco. It is dedicated to the Queen of England. 'The Queens of England are Saints again', Blount writes, 'and the Fruit infinitely great, when People find the way to Heaven, is the way to be well at Court.' He couldn't have written that a year later, with the arrival of Dutch William. He would have had to publish the book abroad, or without a publisher's imprint at all, not openly at Matthew Turner's at the Lamb in High Holborn. This beautiful book cost me half-a-crown at Mr. Gallup's shop on Clapham Common where I bought my Anthony Woods. Mr. Gallup's shop was one of the casualties of the war; it 'went up' on the same day as my house two hundred yards away.

I wish David Low had included an obituary of deaths by bombs or builders. Gone for example is the secondhand bookshop I loved in Westbourne Grove and gone the little bookshop on the triangular site opposite King's Cross Station where I bought *The Adventures* and *The Memoirs of Sherlock Holmes* in their first editions for what seemed then the exorbitant price of £5. That is the sad side of book-hunting; far more shops disappear than new shops open. Even Brighton is not what it was.

GRAHAM GREENE

London Bookshops

By the 1920s, the Charing Cross Road had become 'Books' to the Londoner, and 'the Road' to the booksellers. It had taken the place of the old 'Booksellers' Row' or Holywell Street which had been demolished in 1899 as part of the Aldwych clear-up. From the frontispiece which is a reproduction from a pen-and-ink drawing by Hanslip Fletcher dated 1898, Holywell Street can be seen as running east to west from the present site of Australia House to that of the Gaiety Theatre, with the towers of the Law Courts in the Strand in the background to pin its position. The Hanslip Fletcher drawing has caught the atmosphere of the old Row, with the browsers, including six top hats and morning coats, mixing with cloth caps, bowlers, a little girl in a long pinafore, and a pair of London bobbies. Except for the name, there was not much romance in Booksellers' Row at the end of the century. Narrow and discreet, the late-Victorian 'porno' merchants had been slipping in whenever a shop became vacant. By contrast, the displaced, legitimate booksellers must have found the new Charing Cross Road all sweetness and light, and very grand. At the same time, 'Autolycus of the Bookstalls' was writing in his column in the *Daily News* on the new look in the Charing Cross Road: 'Wanting its bookstalls, this would be one of the most cheerless of metropolitan thoroughfares, with its barrack-like Buildings.'

While the booksellers may have found more air and sun in the Charing Cross Road, they found trouble too: the famous Battle of the Bookstalls. It started in December 1900, when each of the booksellers received a typewritten letter from John Hunt, town clerk to the City Council of Westminster, requesting them to

remove the projecting shelves outside their shop, as these consti-
tuted obstructions and were illegal. The story of the battle is
given in an eight-page supplement to Bertram Dobell's *One
Hundredth Catalogue* (1901). Bertram Dobell was already in the
Charing Cross Road before the new wave, and now offered
himself as the booksellers' champion. He was prosecuted under
the Metropolitan Police Act of 1839, subsection 7, appeared at
Marlborough Street, and was fined one shilling. The booksellers
had lost, and the obstructions are still there.

Of the support which he received, Mr. Dobell quoted from the
Daily Telegraph of 10 January 1901: 'It is interesting to note that
bookstalls existed in Charing Cross Road, although under a
different name, nearly a hundred years ago. It was then known as
Castle Street, but was renamed when the new road was built
fifteen years ago. Quaritch once kept a bookstall in the neighbour-
hood, and round his shop many eminent statesmen, all bouquinistes, were to be seen bending over the ill-kept piles of books,
seeking out some priceless treasure of literature. Even nowadays
such well-known persons as the Home Secretary (Mr. C. T.
Ritchie), Mr. Lecky, M.P., Sir Henry Irving, Mr. Augustine
Birrell, Mr. John Burns, and Mrs. Humphrey Ward spend many
an hour inspecting the books in the fourpenny box. The late
Mr. Gladstone was a frequent customer of the bookstall keepers.
He devoted much time scrutinising old books with dilapidated
covers that had been neglected by seekers after more modern
literature. More than once he has gone away after a long search
with quite a big armful of books. Many famous books have been
picked up from the stalls in Charing Cross Road by men whose one
hobby is to collect old books that possess some literary value. The
State Library of Congress, the Capitol, Washington, contains
many books that have been purchased direct from the bookstalls
of Charing Cross Road, which has now become the favourite
haunt of the bouquinistes of London.'

From an article in *The Times* of the same year on the romance
of the old bookstalls, and on the possibilities latent in the fourpenny box, Mr. Dobell also quotes 'A Browning of the future

may still find his "Book" of books in a booth at Florence and a lira makes it his. Statesmen may still foregather on the quays of Paris and forget their dissensions for the nonce in a common sympathy over the fourpenny box. But Bumble has decreed it otherwise in London, and if he has his way, the fourpenny box will soon know its place no more. . . . Snuffy Davie bought from a stall in Holland for two groschen, or twopence of our money, *Caxton's Game of Chess*, 1474; how this inimitable windfall was first sold for twenty pounds; how it was next sold for seventy pounds; and finally how this finest treasure blazed forth in its full value, and was bought by Royalty itself for one hundred and seventy pounds—could a copy occur now, Lord only knows what would be its ransom.'

Today, the Charing Cross Road, with help from Cecil Court, is still the popular centre of the secondhand book business, much as it was fifty years ago. The difference between the central London book scene of today and of the twenties, is not so much in Charing Cross Road, but in the two areas it separates—the West End and Holborn. The West End of the twenties was that of the great houses of Quaritch, Maggs, Sotheran, Hatchard's, Francis Edwards, Pickering and Chatto, Ellis, and Bumpus, much as it is today. But concentrated just to the east of Charing Cross Road and in Holborn, there were in the twenties four times this number of bookshops. Most were specialists in their particular field, and with the exception of Walter T. Spencer in New Oxford Street, and Batsford's in High Holborn, were run by their owners and one or two assistants. Together they gave London the sort of cohesive book heart-land, which with today's soaring rents, and disappearing books, it is never likely to see again. Even without detailed documentation of the earlier colony of bookshops round St. Paul's, and Dr. Johnson's cluster, it does seem probable that this concentration was unique in the history of English antiquarian bookselling.

Among these Holborn and Bloomsbury booksellers, James Tregaskis and Son at the Sign of the Caxton Head (66 Great Russell Street), were the most venerable; Batsford's at 94 High Holborn already almost a household word; Charles J. Sawyer at 23 New Oxford Street, the most up and coming; Grafton & Co., 51 Great Russell Street, with their learned knockabout turn of the massive Peddie and Fanny Hamel, the most amusing; and Walter T. Spencer, the most impressive and frightening. His business is now moved to Upper Berkeley Street, W1, and with the old man's right hand, Miss Nellie Clark, still in command. Miss Clark does not frighten, one is just staggered by her knowledge, and fascinated by her stories and memories of the old shop in New Oxford Street, with the windows piled with Dickens, Thackeray, Trollope, and Lever in the original monthly parts, each tied in pink tape. The waving coloured background of Gillray, Cruikshank, Australian, and American aquatint views. The Victorian abracadabra in the corners. Inside it was a cavern to match the wealth of the two windows. Shelves of books and folders up to the ceiling, and later one was to know that this was repeated on the two floors above. Under the hissing of the gas, a staff of young women were sorting and pulling out these hundreds of folders. It looked chaotic, but there was complete central control of every folder, with these young women able to produce 'Americana', 'Australiana', 'Sporting', 'Literary', or whatever the collectors coming from all over the world, might ask to see. The full, rich, Walter Spencer story is in his *Forty Years in My Bookshop*, published in 1923, now out of print, but surely due for a reprinting? Here is the story of two great episodes in book collecting—that of the nineteenth-century literary authors in the original parts of their works as published monthly, and of the colour plate book, with the sketches of the collectors who sat in the little Spencer parlour at the back of the shop—the Lords Rosebery and Derby, the wealthy, the English and American, the librarians from all over the world.

Of Mr. Spencer's nearest neighbours, the firm of Charles J. Sawyer moved out of 23 New Oxford Street in 1922, and R. Fletcher moved in from Porchester Road, Bayswater. Sawyer's went to Grafton Street, W1, and are still there, though at a different number. Bill Fletcher eventually settled in Cecil Court, where for fifteen years he was my very good neighbour. Today, with young Keith more and more in the picture, the old firm is very happily set for its third generation.

Mr. Myers I did not meet in his Holborn days, only later, when he was in New Bond Street, and had come down to Cecil Court to wish a beginner well. Today it is difficult to imagine a West End bookseller expending such time and spirit. Happily the same generosity is being carried on by his daughter, Miss Winifred Myers—number one among English dealers in autographs and manuscript material.

Furthest east along Holborn, old Mr. Redway had his Frank Hollings bookshop in the Great Turnstile. The quietest and most discriminating of these booksellers, he specialized in the Kelmscott and the lesser contemporary private press work, with an unexpected sideline in books on chess. Today, the Frank Hollings bookshop is still further to the east, in Cloth Fair, and part of Bertram Rota Ltd.

Batsford's were the most solid of the High Holborn bookshops; first at No. 52, with a move to No. 94 in 1893, then west to North Audley Street in 1930, on to Fitzhardinge Street in 1957, and now part of Blackwell's, Oxford. Solid also were Walford Brothers, in these days the firm for genealogists and county historians. And if Walford Brothers could not come up with the book, there was Buchanan's across Holborn at the corner of Lincoln's Inn Fields. But even then Holborn solidity had its fringe. In Featherstone Buildings, just off High Holborn, there was Mr. Weir, a taciturn Scot with a shop full of *Vanity Fair* cartoons and nothing else. He sat in the shop window all day, writing endless letters, smoking endless pipes, and looking awkward. Much more cheerful was Frank Archer's bookshop round the corner in Red Lion Street. This was the bookshop supplying the *avant garde* of the twenties and thirties with their reading, but more important a meeting place when 'The Plough' and 'The Fitzroy Tavern' were closed. Less cheerful, almost macabre, was the Catholic bookshop run by the Caldwell father and son in Red Lion Passage. Inexplicable rather than mysterious was Mr. Jenkins's bookshop in Sicilian

Avenue. A pleasant man, with a pleasant stock among which I never remember seeing one tempting book. Somehow, his bookshop seemed very much part of this tesselated Bloomsbury-Italianate gesture which has never tidied in with the London scene.

It was, however, round the British Museum, in Museum Street, Great and Little Russell Streets, that London in the twenties and thirties came anywhere near having a book quarter after the style of Paris's Sixième Quartier. From east to west along Great Russell Street, first, James Tregaskis and Son, at No. 66, with the proud title at the Sign of the Caxton Head, witness to its literary tradition. On the opposite corner the tall, ruddy, Scandinavian descended, George Salby, specialist in Archaeology, Anthropology, Greek, and Middle East. There were too many folios which could not be shelved, so they either piled round the shop, or fell across the windows. Neither Mr. Salby nor the professors coming across from their work in the Museum bothered about this. He was, however, fussy about the string and the paper in which his purchases arrived. These would be carefully put on one side to be used in his own outgoings. Next door bar one, George Harding's bookshop for History, mainly English. Mr. Harding had just died, leaving the business to his old manager, Mr. Wheeler, whose particular interests were the pamphlets and periodicals of the English Radicals in the nineteenth century. To this day, collectors and librarians at the institutes for sociological studies now appearing all over the country, speak about old man Wheeler's legendary collection. The old Thackeray Hotel stood in between George Harding's bookshop and the Coptic House of Grafton & Co. As publishers of *The Library*, and other bibliographical monographs, Bibliography was their line, but it is as the pioneer in the new collecting, what is now called 'Industrial Archaeology', that Grafton's and Mr. Peddie will be remembered. Peddie had come from the St. Bride's Library of Printing to join with Miss Fanny Hamel in the most uneasy, ill-assorted, and happiest of partnerships. They were both in their late sixties when I met them.

Peddie ran the antiquarian side, he rarely bought in the rooms because Miss Hamel carried on about prices she thought too high, so it was from his regular Saturday morning visits to the book barrows in the Farringdon Road, and from an army of faithful old book runners that he picked up the 'inconsiderables', which *en masse* built up the most original stock in London. Miss Hamel took charge of administration. About the beginning of the century, as 'Frank Hamel' she had written, and Eveleigh Nash had published, several lives of French marquises of the eighteenth century. Now she wore a red wig, and chased the staff. Whenever there were tears, the victim was sent for a nice walk round the British Museum block. At closing time, they were let out at intervals because Miss Hamel thought that gossiping at the door was ill-bred. When the girls left to get married, they would come back to show Miss Hamel their families. The men assistants left to open their own shops, and here too, there was always goodwill on both sides. Between them, Peddie and Miss Hamel apprenticed more good booksellers than any other London bookshop.

Next along Great Russell Street were the three Oriental specialists, Kegan Paul, Luzac, and Probsthain, still there today, but their Oriental lure never tempted in quite the way that Grafton's did. For a year or so in the late twenties, there had been 'The Ulysses Bookshop' squeezed in between these Orientalists. The owner was Dr. Jacob Schwartz from the U.S.A. I first heard about him from the porters at Hodgson's who used to walk round London with the sales catalogues, and who had been fascinated by the garrett in High Holborn at which they delivered the Schwartz copy. It was then that Jake Schwartz issued his 'spoof' catalogue, now a rarity. Along with some items which he considered serious, there were the bookseller's fashionables which Jake priced at what he considered the right price, with notes about contemporary *bêtises*. We used to meet at Hodgson's, but I never found him at home in 'The Ulysses Bookshop'. Here it was usually Annie, Jake's Bloomsbury charlady who had an appropriate touch of Mrs. Bloom in her chatter. I remember her semi-withering, semi-envious comments on the flattened springs which she showed me in the couch in the bookshop.

The next, and last bookshop in Great Russell Street, that of Henry Stevens, Son and Stiles at No. 39, was the most significant not only among this group, but in the English–American antiquarian book trade. The Henry Stevens, then senior partner in these twenties, was the son of a notable bookseller and bibliographer, Henry Stevens of Vermont. The father had come over to London in 1845, and started business as an antiquarian bookseller at 4 Trafalgar Square. The young Henry joined his father in 1880, and on the father's death in 1886, moved the business up to Great Russell Street, where it was to remain till the late move to Farnham, Surrey, in 1963. Americana of every sort, books, atlases, charts, and views, was his province. No bookseller handled, and is now likely to handle, the quantity and quality he did. No bookseller will ever know more about this subject. On his death in 1930, Mr. G. F. Barwick, of the British Museum, in an official tribute, thanked him for the opportunities he always gave to that institution for the buying of so many important additions. On his last visit to the States in 1923, the University of Michigan made him an honorary M.A. An Antiquarian Booksellers' Association was something he had always worked for, and when it was finally established at a public meeting of secondhand booksellers at the Criterion Restaurant on 11 December 1906, as the Association of Second-Hand Booksellers, Mr. Henry N. Stevens was elected as its first annual President.

Little Russell Street was more modest with two bookshops only, but with the First Edition Club to help out. No two bookshops could have been more different. B. F. Stevens and Brown Ltd., with their large warehouse at 28–30 Little Russell Street, and the largest library commitments in the secondhand book trade, and the Macleish Brothers who had just moved up from the Aldwych to a house six doors away. The Macleishes were two of the most modest and likeable men in the trade. They specialized in English Literature and issued catalogues after the style of Pickering and Chatto, and Percy Dobell, and they had a devoted following among American university librarians. The First Edition Club, then in decline, was just opposite them in part of the presbytery of St. George's, Bloomsbury, but such goings on were not after their style, and they were amused when I said that I thought of joining. I did call to get a membership form from A. J. A. Symons. He was busy discussing biblio-esoteric problems with Christopher Millard (the 'Stuart Mason' bibliographer of Oscar Wilde), and the more intense the discussion, the more certain one was, that it must be membership of the Macleish Gang, rather than of the First Edition Club.

Museum Street may have had only four bookshops, but in their fire-power, two were London's leading marksmen. Raphael King had hardly left school, when he was joining in at the book auctions, beating up the prices of books he felt were undervalued, and beating his elders too. He died just after the last war, having helped to add an overdue revaluation of the first editions of books whose publication was a milestone along some road. Before his interest turned to first editions in the scientific fields, he had concentrated on modern first editions, and I remember being grateful, when at a Hodgson sale in 1928, he paid £22 for the copy of Bernard Shaw's *Widowers' Houses* I had picked up in Berlin that summer for eight marks.

Across Museum Street, Leon Kashnor's Museum Book Store concentrated on one field only, Social and Economic History. Unlike Raphael, he did not bother with the auction rooms. Either he or his scouts knew, and were friends with, most of the country booksellers, particularly with those in the north. The early English Radical periodicals and ephemera were what he liked most. He was among the first of the booksellers to wait till they had made a large collection round some movement or man. There can be few big American university libraries without one of his collections. Like Henry Stevens, no other bookseller is likely to know more about his own subject since none is ever likely to see or handle the quantity and quality of books which these two did.

If Davis and Orioli, then at 30 Museum Street, did not have the panache of Raphael King and Leon Kashnor, they had scholarship and background; Cambridge for Irving Davis, and Florence for Orioli. Their bookshop was in the best Museum tradition.

The fourth Museum Street bookseller was a cheerful American, Paul B. Victorius, working like Raphael King and Leon Kashnor from an office on the first floor. First editions of nineteenth-century scientific works were his enthusiasm. At the beginning of the war he went back to America and a shop in Charlottesville. He was a change from conventional subject areas, helping the less travelled booksellers of these days to understand the American style.

If the Holborn of today is complete 'book loss' to what it was in the twenties, Bloomsbury is both loss and improvement, with two spectacular transformations. When Henry Stevens, Son and Stiles moved out of 39 Great Russell Street and down to Farnham, my old friend Ben Weinreb moved in, and the shop which Henry Stevens had made number one for Americana in the book-selling world, within a few years became another number one as B. Weinreb Architectural Books Ltd. Two years ago, as part of, and in tune with this Architecture, Weinreb and Douwma Ltd. took over 93 Great Russell Street from the Dryad Press and craft shop, transforming this large corner site into the most attractive print shop in London. In the late thirties, Miss Una Dillon opened a modest bookshop in Store Street. Everyone liked her, and most people were sorry for her chances in this antiquarian male rumble tumble. Today, I only wish that there were more oldtimers left to see Dillon's University Bookshop, 1 Malet Street, with its twenty rooms on four floors, its lift, and reputation as the finest university bookshop in the country.

Stanley Crowe's bookshop at 5 Bloomsbury Street is a third transformation story, but one known to few, and very different from those of Ben Weinreb and Miss Dillon.

During the last war the large basement at 5 Bloomsbury Street was one of the air-raid shelters looked after by the wardens of Holborn Post No. 1, with its H.Q. in the basement of the London School of Hygiene and Tropical Medicine in Gower Street. As an air-raid warden, this was one of the shelters on our twice-nightly inspections. We went out in pairs, and whenever possible Warden Cole and I, having been friends in happier days, went

out together. 'Little Cole' was one of the best of the London
book runners, dragging parcels of books from one bookshop to
some other whom he thought likely to fall for them. He used to
come to my shop to have a rest, and rub out tell-tale prices in the
books he was running around. One almost enjoyed these patrols
with him, because he was having the time of his life. There was a
uniform, a regular wage for a job with some possible danger, but
with lots of time for darts at the post, inter-post darts matches,
Tommy Handley on the non-stop wireless, intrigues and jeal-
ousies among the full-time wardens, gossip about the part-time
ones. He was able to keep up his book running during the afternoons, and tell me about the literary 'killings' and the disasters in
the nights. The A.R.P. was not only doing all this for him, but it
seemed to have mapped out a bright future too. Graham Greene
was also one of our part-timers. Little Cole had a great admiration
for him, also a brilliant idea. With Cole's knowledge of all the
tricks and tricksters in the antiquarian book trade, and Graham
Greene knowing all about writing and writers, 'Cole and Greene'
would be an unstoppable combination once the war was over.
But before it was over, Graham had left Post No. 1 for Intelli-
gence, after the war the Cole family were rehoused in a fine new
house in a model satellite town, and little Cole hated it. The
A.R.P. also gave Cole and me a common interest in that air-
raid shelter at 5 Bloomsbury Street which appeared on the Post
record, night after night, with one occupant only. He was a
middle-aged Pole, and with one of his sidelines in old books, Cole
was one of his special friends. I do not think, however, that it was
the books so much as the shared understanding that these were
the happiest years of both of their lives. The Pole had trouble at
home and only went back for an occasional bath. In the corner of
the shelter, he had a camp stool and bed, an oil stove for his tea,
a handful of books, and the visits of the wardens. When Stanley
Crowe came back from the war, his old shop in Sise Lane in the
City had been blitzed, and he went to the small shop upstairs and
our enormous A.R.P. basement at 5 Bloomsbury Street. There
was no Pole now in the corner, and soon with the cascade from

Sotheby's and Hodgson's, there was hardly room for a perch.
Today, Stanley has the finest stock of English topographical books
ever got together by a bookseller, and this with the memory of
the old stocks of the Walford brothers, and of Bernard Halliday
of Leicester. There is a regular series of catalogues, and almost
miraculously the business hums along, with only Stanley and Mary
to keep it going. When Stanley is at the sales, Mary is alone in the
caverns, and one is a warden once again, only this time there is no
need for cheering up—Mary has ten tons of books around her.

The bookshops in the Charing Cross Road as one of London's
'You're sure to find it there', have always had a brisk cash business,
and little time for the glories and follies of Holborn and Bloomsbury. As the writer in the *Daily News* prophesied in 1899, when
they moved in from Holywell Street, they would be giving
colour and warmth to 'the most cheerless main thoroughfare in
London', and this they continue to give. And first, E. Joseph at
48a, because Mr. and Mrs. Joseph were among the first settlers,
and their sons, Jack and Sam, still run the business today. Still also
perfectly able to give and take with the best and the very much
younger in the trade, and with a grandson, the young David, a
happy and worthy chip to see that the old business goes on and on.

At the top end of the road was the house of Marks, related by
marriage to the Joseph family, and for the forty years I knew it,
always seeming the most complete bookshop in the road. The
basement, with its shelves of library bindings, among which one
might spot the book that counted in its own right. The ground
floor, with cloth for the browsers, and Benny Marks reading *The
Times* at the end. I never saw him doing anything else. He would
look up with a little smile, 'Hello! old chap, you know your way
about, carry on', and he would carry on with his *Times*. On the
first floor, there were library sets, handsomely bound, with the
glass cases for standard and expensive first editions; on the second
floor Freemasonry and less obvious Rariora. The third floor had
a notice across the stairs 'Private', which was an apology for the
confusion. Topographical literature was the theme here, but that
seemed to include the many books and pamphlets about which no

one could quite make up his mind as to where they belonged, or how they should be priced. This was the floor Benny Marks knew I was going to, though it was to his partner, Mark Cohen, that I had to go for the reckoning. It was the fairest, no-nonsense bookshop I ever knew. It closed two years ago, partly because of the deaths of Benny Marks and the faithful manager, Frank Doel, but mainly because of the overheads in a main thoroughfare. How could a shop with three floors and a basement survive on the sale of individual books, while its neighbours were turning over paperbacks, piano accordions, or suits of clothes as fast as they could get them? I am glad that in her *84, Charing Cross Road*, Miss Helene Hanff has written the memorial to a bookshop which, knowing all about its books, was sometimes perplexed about its customers, especially about this lady from New York, but in the end was to respond as warmly as she had begun the correspondence.

In between Messrs. Joseph and Marks on the east side of the road were the troopers. At No. 52, old George Winter, who unlike his neighbours continued to issue a series of over one hundred catalogues right up to the thirties.

At No. 56, Mr. A. H. Mayhew, another exception, with scholarly interests. Between 1924 and 1929, he published an edition of *The Wayland-Dietrich Saga*, edited by his friend, Mrs. Katherine M. Buck. Like most secondhand booksellers who become publishers, he learned that love wasn't quite enough [*et tu* Emmington?].

At No. 64, Mr. F. B. Neumayer, the gentlest bookseller in the road. At the beginning of the First World War, he had been in partnership with his brother-in-law, Mr. E. Weyhe; both had been born in Germany. Eventually Mr. Weyhe left for New York, where in Lexington Avenue he built up what is still America's leading Fine Arts bookshop. Mr. Neumayer stayed here, carrying on till his death just after the end of the last war, with art books of a less flamboyant style. Without disrespect, one thought of him as the 'poor man's Zwemmer'. Mr. Zwemmer had not yet come to give real distinction to Charing Cross Road with his bookshop at No. 78, and his gallery in Litchfield Street.

In the centre of the Road, the most cheerful and typical of the Charing Cross Road troopers, the two Jackson brothers, with no recondite book rarity nonsense, nor catalogues. Charles was at No. 50, and Albert Jackson at No. 68. Charles, a stout elderly man, I never saw other than slouched on his chair just inside the door. He left the running of the business to his son, and to Fred and Bert, two splendid Cockneys. On their way to a sale, or just down to the 'Salisbury' pub for a drink, they used to call in at Cecil Court. They knew nothing about books, but all about prices, especially the profitable sales at the lesser auction rooms in and about London, where twenty to fifty lots of books might be included among some miscellaneous property, and certainly all that was happening in the Road. If it wasn't bibliography, it was very relaxed, only the shag which they smoked hung about our shop for hours. Young Jackson was killed in the war, and his old father closed the shop.

A happier story at the other Jackson shop, No. 68, 'Albert Jackson and Son', where old Charles's nephew Richard was in charge. The original Albert Jackson had started the bookshop in Great Portland Street in 1873, then after a couple of years in Albany Street, NW1, his son Richard brought it to 68 Charing Cross Road in 1910. He died in 1924, and it was now his son Richard who was in charge. Today, this Richard only comes up twice a week, a little bemused by the changes in the Road which he has known for sixty-one years, and leaves the running of the business to his son Bryan. Bryan tells me that during school holidays, one of his small son's treats is coming up for an afternoon in his dad's shop, so a fifth generation for 'Albert Jackson and Son' seems likely. When first writing about Albert Jackson's bookshop, I had also written about their assistant Albert Thompson, who had come to the shop straight from school, just after the First World War, and fifty-four years later was still there. Before these recollections were finished, a sad note from Bryan Jackson told he had lost his faithful Albert. So, the mention becomes now both a memory and a tribute to a bookseller's assistant whom I remember for over forty years, with the same gentle smile, during the worst years of the trade depressions of the early thirties, and during the London blitz of the early forties.

But the Road wasn't uniform. Next door but one to Albert Jackson there was Henry Danielson at No. 72, discouraging browsers in his shop and camaraderies with his neighbours. A tall man in a dark suit, never without the bowler which he wore in the shop too, he strode down the Road never seeing anyone. English Literature was his speciality, and in 1921 he had written an excellent bibliography of modern authors. He was an authority on the writers of the nineties, and if it had not been for the bowler, there was Baron Corvo written all over him. Corvine too, the way he lovingly handled his books, and the beautiful pencilling in of the price. If Danielson had a friend in the Road, it was Stanislas, 'Stan' to the other booksellers, and I never discovered if this was his Christian or surname. Stan had started as an assistant in Charing Cross Road, and I had known him with bookshops in Fleet Street, the Tottenham Court Road, and St. Martin's Court, then in 1933 when old George Winter at last retired from No. 52, Stan moved in with his International Bookshop. That lasted two years, and rather late Stan discovered that freelancing from an office in Holborn more suited his Polish blood. His fellow booksellers never quite approved. Then there was Stan's knowledge of French, and the kind of book this led to. I got to know him motoring to some country sales, and liked him. He may have seemed a maverick to the trade, but they had not known his Scottish wife, nor of Stan's love of the Scottish hills. He was delighted that neither of his sons wanted to have anything to do with bookselling!

On the other side of the Road, the west and the wrong side, there were two booksellers almost certainly happy to be on the wrong and quiet side. At No. 77 was Arthur Dobell, in the same shop as his father, the great Bertram Dobell, who had come there in 1884. English Literature was still the only subject he bothered with, but it became more and more difficult for Mr. Dobell to adjust to the very modest changes in the authors that were now favoured, and the prices to be asked in the thirties and forties.

His son was interested in, and became an authority on jazz, and then on pop music. A few gramophone records appeared at the front of the shop, then swelled so that the books began to retreat. The last time I went into the shop, it was only the office at the back which was for books. In the end, No. 77 became number one in London for pop classics.

A few doors down was Cyril Beaumont's Ballet Bookshop. Visits there were mainly to see Mr. Beaumont's mild surprise that anyone could think that there would be any but books on Ballet in his shop, but, at times, there were.

Without Foyles' bookshop, the play of the Charing Cross Road is Hamlet without the Princes in the Tower, but as William and Gilbert Foyle had made their London debut in my Cecil Court, I have claimed their story for the later Cecil Court story.

The bookshop of James Bain Ltd. should not strictly be part of the Charing Cross Road story, but geographically, William IV Street, Strand, is nearer Charing Cross Road than to any other grouping. Following the sweep of the Charing Cross Road south-east, the continuation is William IV Street, where James Bain's bookshop had been at No. 14 for the last 50 of its 150 years in the West End. After the last war, the business was bought by Rodney Drake who has now taken it down to Horsham. If No. 14 is now only a memory, it is one recently stirred when reading *The Letters of C. S. Lewis*. I came across one to his father: 'I have bought an edition of Yeats. In the same shop I'm afraid I gave myself away badly. What first tempted me to go in was a battered copy of Burton's "Anatomy". I went in and asked a courtly old gentleman to let me see it. "H'm," said I, glancing over the dirty old volume, "it seems rather worn; have you a newer copy?" The old gentleman looked at me in rather a pained way and said he had not. "Well, how much is it?" I asked rathr expecting a considerable reduction. "Twenty-five guineas", said my friend with a bland smile. Ye Gods! just think of it! there was I for the first time in my life, fingering a really valuable old edition and asking for a newer copy. I turned hot all over. However, the old gentleman was very forgiving, and turned his treasury inside out for me. Well "ego in Arcadia vixi", and it was something to have been in the shop of James Bain, even for an hour.'

With a touch of C. S. Lewis's lyricism, I too remembered the two courtly old gentlemen sitting in the wide alcove at the end of the long elegant shop; Mr. de Coverley, and Mr. Maine, late librarian at Chatsworth, who had just joined him, both sucking away at their pipes. Between them was the Georgian bookcase holding Doves Press and Kelmscott Press, and seventeenth-century Richard Burtons in more esteemed condition than C. S. Lewis's copy in the window. On the walls were photographs from Mr. Bain's esteemed clients. Today I can only remember one from Richard Monckton Milnes, first Baron Houghton, but it must have been a gallery of the great collectors of the last half of the last century, and of the first quarter of ours. As I had to pass along William IV Street on my way to Barclay's bank in the Strand, these visits were more than C. S. Lewis's occasional rite. The Georgian bookcase and the Doves Press were not for me, but there was a large basement which the old gentlemen had forgotten about. On the top shelves there, which needed a ten-foot ladder, there were rows of the Augustan poets in their dust wrappers, just as they had been put there before the First World War. One felt like a greedy urchin bringing one's find back to the old gentlemen for their indulgent pricing. They were just mildly amused, as they waited patiently for heroes who alas! came less and less. T. E. Lawrence had just gone, Maurice Baring was too frail, but there might be a visit from Hugh Walpole? I still regret not having asked about Henry James. Of all the London book-shops, this surely would have been the one in which he would have felt most at home.

A pedestrian precinct, located strategically between the West End and the City, it seems strange that Cecil Court should have to wait till the thirties before becoming the new Booksellers' Row. It could have happened in 1899, but the booksellers from the old Booksellers' Row preferred Charing Cross Road when their Holywell Street was swept away. Instead of the booksellers, the new film industry moved in, and till the First World War, Cecil Court was 'Flicker Alley'. Geoffrey Watkins, my old neighbour in Cecil Court, tells me that my shop was the office of Nordisk films, with a large portrait of Asta Nielsen, their star, in the window. The J. M. Watkins bookshop, with a world-wide reputation for its books and publications on comparative religion and mysticism was started by Geoffrey's father in Whitehall and moved to Cecil Court in 1900, where it still is today, with No. 19 now added to the original No. 21. In these pre-First World War years there was another bookshop at No. 9, but this was more of a literary salon, run by a bubbling Irishman, Dan Rider, for the Bernard Shaw, Frank Harris circle.

The year 1904, with the arrival of the brothers Foyle, is Cecil Court's *annus mirabilis* which although it went into a Trinity is generally forgotten today. The brothers had started bookselling two years before from their home in north London. The books were first stored in the back kitchen, and when they overflowed into the family dining room they hired a neighbouring warehouse for five shillings a week. The business came from advertisements in local and educational weeklies. They offered textbooks for sale, offering to buy any number themselves, and while sales and offers snowballed, the brothers hankered for more than this postal business. They wanted to be real booksellers with a real shop, so they moved across London to a small shop in Peckham, where with an unfurnished room round the corner to live in, they were really out on their own. Over the door of the shop, they painted in gilt letters 'With all Faith', and they never stopped working, on Sundays too. But Peckham had drawbacks. It meant too much cycling for William up and down to central London, because to be sure of quick deliveries he used to ride up to the General Post Office each evening with the morning orders. Now, with a shop, they were meeting customers, but Peckham people were not enough. They reconnoitred about the City, then around the West End, eventually deciding that the ideal compromise was Cecil Court in WC2. There was a small shop, No. 16, vacant at a rent of £60 a year, and they took it. William was then

aged 19 and Gilbert 18. A year later they took on their first
assistant who went off with the weekly takings. Two years later
they felt that even Cecil Court was not enough; they would now
take on their rivals round the corner in the great Charing Cross
Road itself. There was a fine shop empty, No. 135, and they
rented it with a fourteen-year lease. There is a privately printed
history of the firm (*The Romance of a Bookshop, 1904-1929*),
written in 1929, by Gilbert Fabes, who was then manager of the
Rare Book Department. As interesting as Mr. Fabes's facts was
his glowing announcement of the firm's imminent move into the
new additional premises in Manette Street: 'In this new building,
erected on the site of the Old Goldbeater's House, there will be a
floor area of 30,000 square feet, with accommodation for two
million volumes, two lifts and a lecture hall.' That was the story
of the first twenty-five years of the Foyles' Bookshop. Today I
wonder what my old friend would have managed for these following forty-four years? I called on him in the Rare Book Department
in the late twenties, just after he had made his favourite buy,
Bernard Shaw's surplus books (on his move from the Adelphi to
the more compact flat in Whitehall Court). And today, I still have
the Beardsley print I bought from the Shaw collection. Years later,
when he had left Foyle's and was in his own bookshop in the old
High Street in Rye, Gilbert was to buy another and more literary
library. Henry James's 'Lamb House' had been badly damaged in
an air raid during the war, and Gilbert was brought in to save
what could be saved. The books he bought appeared in his three
catalogues, Nos. 17-19, 1949-51. When the old High Street
became too bustling, Gilbert went into semi-retirement in a
wooden house on Winchelsea beach. An old railway carriage was
added for a bookroom. Nothing could have been more different
from the Foyle story, but as one sat with Gilbert in the old railway
carriage between the sea and the marsh, his did seem the ideal last
years for any, and all 'loners'.

Of the Foyles' Cecil Court years, two recent reminders. The
very kind letter to me from William's daughter Christina: 'My
father opened his shop in Cecil Court in 1904, and I think he must

have moved to the Charing Cross Road in about 1906. He was always such a fanatic about books and work that he quickly built up a very big mail order business, and so many letters came to the little shop in Cecil Court that the police raided him thinking that he was carrying on an illegal betting business. When they saw that this young man of nineteen was working so hard to find books for students, they helped him in many ways by recommending everyone to him, and he built up a wonderful goodwill. My mother had a bookshop in New Oxford Street. She was only a girl, and my father persuaded her to join him in Cecil Court. It was a very romantic story.' And from Geoffrey Watkins, whose father's bookshop was opposite that of the Foyles': 'A few years after the last war, Willy Foyle dropped in for a chat, and said something to the effect—"Funny to remember that your father lent me the money on more than one occasion to pay my staff wages. It probably wasn't much, and I would like to have to pay it now."'

Before Cecil Court became a booksellers' row, one other name that could be squeezed in, Thomas Thorp. Mr. Thorp had the large corner shop in the Court with the door in St. Martin's Lane, and thus so addressed, but the three large windows looked into Cecil Court, and it was these windows that were to remain the Thorp legend. For years after I opened in Cecil Court they used to be quoted, first with 'Prices marked inside', then 'All at two shillings', followed by 'One shilling', and the final wild 'Sixpenny' scramble. Mr. Thorp was there for a few years at the end of the twenties, went to Guildford in 1932, reappearing in a very grand shop at the end of Old Bond Street until the outbreak of the last war. The eldest son Tom then went to Jermyn Street and on to Albemarle Street, where he still is. The younger son Hugh remained in Guildford, where he too is still at the top of the High Street, in a shop modest enough from the front, but with a corridor leading into an ex-Nonconformist chapel stuffed with the most riotous choc-a-bloc of books in the antiquarian book trade.

Thomas Thorp's was the last of Cecil Court's *fausses Pointes du Jour*. In 1933 it became the bouquiniste quartier that the book correspondent of *The Times* of 1899 looked forward to seeing in London, and he would have been happy to know that it still is that today. First there was my oldest bookseller friend, Harold Edwards. After leaving Hodgson's in the spring, I had been looking for a bookshop during that summer, and a shop in Cecil Court, rent £125 a year, seemed the answer. It may have been double what the Foyles were faced with in 1904, but like them, one felt that the Court doubled the value in its strategic position. Doubly reassured too when taking possession in September 1933 to find that Harold Edwards, later to be President of the Antiquarian Booksellers' Association, had moved into the shop almost opposite six weeks earlier. Today after our Cecil Court apprenticeship, we are separated, not by the width of the Court, but by thirty miles along the Icknield Way, he in wilder Berkshire, and I in wildest Oxfordshire. No two booksellers can have a pleasanter way of communicating than along the old Icknield Way, first under the Chilterns, across the Thames where a bridge takes the place of the old ford, up over the eastern spur of the Wantage Downs, and the drop into Hermitage and Ashmore Green. Both the getting there and the returning seem to add a blessing to the biblio-brotherhood already inwardly blessed by Olive, 'Mrs. Beeton supremo' among booksellers' wives.

Après Harold *et moi*, it was very soon *le Dèluge* in Cecil Court, with Justin Clarke-Hall's the next bookshop (today in Bride Court). Then the Dolphin Book Company, still the only bookshop in the country for Spanish books, today old friends and neighbours in less wild Oxfordshire, Cumnor. Harold Storey followed, and his son Norman is still in his father's old shop. Mr. Seligmann, specialist in Fine Art books, is still there. H. M. Fletcher also, with the third generation (Keith Fletcher) ensuring continuity. During my twenty-three years in the Court, there were about twenty comings, stayings, and goings, and Peter Murray Hill's was finest. He had first come into my shop one evening in 1937, and asked if we could do a deal with, say, fifty miscellaneous books for his stall in the Caledonian Market, that now fabulous forerunner of the Portobello Road antiquarian market. Next morning he called for the books in an old Bentley. The vintage Bentley and the old vintage Caledonian Market suited Peter and his story. After Cambridge he was meant for his father's firm of solicitors in the City, which he hated, and left as soon as he decently could. For a short spell he joined the Edinburgh repertory company which was a relief except for the salary, but this he was able to make up at poker. The Newcastle upon Tyne repertory company came next, and then the beautiful redhead, whom he was always talking about, and whom later, one was to know as Phyllis Calvert, and Peter's wife. From Newcastle, Peter went to the Old Vic and some disenchantment with the stage and its folk. He was sharing a flat with another actor in the company, Peter du Callion, and on one of their rummagings around the old Caledonian Market came 'Blow the old girl [Lilian Baylis], let's have a pitch too, but books, not bric-à-brac'. They both enjoyed their Tuesdays there, and then big Peter became enthusiastic, and serious, for the first time in his life about business. When I told them that a small shop in the Court was about to be empty and the rent £90 a year, they moved in. Six months later the larger shop next to mine also became empty, and they moved into No. 15. Till the war put an end to side-shows, the two Peters stage-managed in Cecil Court the brightest of biblio. pantomimes. There were plenty of books knocking around in those days, but big Peter was impatient to see more. I remember a thirty-shilling return night trip to Edinburgh for the rugby international, also a similar trip over to Dublin for the horse show. We did not see any rugby or horses, but came home with a great many parcels. And that was the foundation of Peter Murray Hill (Books) Ltd.

After the war Peter was joined for a few years by Arnold Muirhead, one of his admired collector customers. Today, Arnold continues as one of my oldest customers and friends. Visits to him at St. Albans having the added pleasure and nostalgia that sixty years ago Mrs. Muirhead and I were creeping to neighbouring academies in our native Glasgow. England is very full of homesick Scots, sick too at any thought of returning north, but much comforted by such get-togethers.

17 Cecil Court,
1950

Emmington,
1960

Summer in
Emmington,
1972

The Murray Hill Bookshop is still in Sloane Avenue, and still issuing some of the best catalogues of seventeenth- and eighteenth-century English literature in the book trade, and with Martin Hamlyn, Peter's completely right successor and the owner of the business, being this year's President of the Antiquarian Booksellers' Association just as Peter himself was in 1956–7. His tragically early death so soon after his year of Presidency was a deep personal loss which many of us still feel.

In the West End today are most of the great names as they were in the twenties, although most with different addresses. Two immovables however—Messrs. Francis Edwards Ltd., and the House of Hatchard's.

Hatchard's first as the senior, i.e. founded on 1 July 1797 by the original John with his capital of £5. The first shop was at 173 Piccadilly, a few doors west of the present No. 187. When he died in 1849, John Hatchard was worth £100,000, and the most respected bookseller in London. One of his earliest customers had been the Duke of Wellington, and almost the whole of the Victorian establishment was to follow. Palmerston, Peel, Gladstone, Lords Salisbury, Derby, and Macaulay. As bookseller-publisher, John Hatchard got a larger public for the ideas of his friends in the Clapham Sect; Wilberforce, Sir Thomas Bernard, Zachary Macaulay, and Hannah More.

The second great Hatchard's phase was that of A. L. Humphreys. Arthur Humphreys became a junior assistant in October 1881 at £1 a week. Ten years later, he was a partner in the firm which he left in 1924. It was at that time, when freelancing among the nobility, and bringing down their books to be sold at Hodgson's, that I met Arthur Humphreys. Burly, bowler-hatted, usually with a violet shirt, high starch collar, and black tie, and manners varying from the most gracious to blank unseeing, but he had seen a lot of top Edwardian life. He had helped Lady Brook, Edward VII's Daisy, Countess of Warwick, build up her library of books on gardens and aristocratic memoirs. He had been the confidant of Cecil Rhodes for his library at Groote Schur. He had been consultant to the lordly libraries at Knowsley, Chevening

(Lord Stanhope's), Mar Lodge (the Duke of Fife's), Syston Park, Grantham. Debrett tripped daily into his office, and among his literati were Rudyard Kipling, George Moore, Ronald Firbank, Richard le Gallienne, and Mrs. Humphrey Ward. Oscar Wilde's last visit was when he came in with Lord Alfred Douglas the day before the production of *The Importance of Being Earnest*. It may not have been the book world of Lords Spencer or Houghton, Henry E. Huntington, Bernard Quaritch, or Tregaskis, but between them John Hatchard and Arthur Humphreys were exactly right as book advisers to Victorian worth and Edwardian gilt.

In the thirties when I used to go to the Rare Book Department on the first floor, a Mr. Jewers was in charge. He was a discreet sober man, who sometimes reminisced, recalling the visits of Queen Mary, or the Royal dukes coming to him for advice, and buying colour plate books. His assistant was a most cheerful, down-to-earth ex-petty officer. If only King George V had been more of a Piccadilly book man, here would have been the assistant after his heart.

After the last war, it seemed that there might be another spectacular Hatchard phase. During his years in prison, the financier Clarence Hatry had learned the comfort of books. On his release, he turned to bookselling, and to what he considered the best bookshop in London. He persuaded an old colleague of mine at Hodgson's, J. G. Millward, to come and manage the Rare Book Department. From Millward one heard about the ambitions, but somehow the new phase never got off the ground, and Hatchard's became once again, the steady Piccadilly Book Man.

Second of the great immovables, Francis Edwards Ltd., is still at 83 Marylebone High Street, and the Rock of Gibraltar among English bookshops. Established in 1826 by a Mr. G. Stockley, the business went, in 1855, to Mr. Francis Edwards who had married Mr. Stockley's daughter. Francis Edwards then moved to the present address in Marylebone High Street in 1860, dying in 1875, when his place was taken by his 15-year-old son, the second Francis Edwards, who was to carry on for the next sixty-nine years (active, and full of business) right up to his death in December 1944. The obituary issued by the firm showed not only the breadth of his interests, but also the personal attention he brought to them all. His customers and friends ranged from Wilkie Collins, Bulwer Lytton, Lord Asquith, and Earl Grey to John Burns and A. E. Newton. The famous libraries which owed more to him than to any other bookseller were: the Turnbull (New Zealand), the Mitchell (New South Wales), and the Mendelssohn (South Africa). Then there was the new bookshop, built in 1912, and still today the most pleasantly designed bookshop anywhere, with the fine bookcases in the front shop with their rich morocco and calf gilt sets, the view into the long light gallery beyond with the massed ranks and shelves, and the lift going up to the more mysterious floors above. Yet with all its size and great reputation, there is the personal touch about Francis Edwards Ltd., probably stemming from the long reign of the second Mr. Francis, and still carried on by directors and staff.

Weightiest of the movings during this period was that of the great house of Bernard Quaritch Ltd., after sixty-two years in Grafton Street, driven out by the inexorable developers. Not again, the climb up the solid staircase to the smaller rooms, less calf and morocco gilded than the ground floor, but still with the aura of the days when Number One among English booksellers opened his first shop at 16 Castle Street, Leicester Square. Today, the great house is less than a mile away at 5–8 Lower John Street, in a building more than a mile from the Grafton Street style. Professor Nikolaus Pevsner writes about it in the London volume of *The Buildings of England*, 'In Lower John Street, an oddly grand mid-Victorian façade of remarkably consistent design, white brick, thirteen bays with gaunt giant pilasters and very long thin windows; the middle window round-headed through one-and-a-half floors. It was apparently from the beginning no more than a warehouse.' To which *Recording Quaritch* rightly adds 'but a treasure house indeed'.

In 1936 there had been another move among the fortress houses—Henry Sotheran Ltd. from 43 Piccadilly to the present 2–5 Sackville Street.

Originally a Yorkshire firm, the first Mr. Henry Sotheran had a bookshop in York during the 1760s. The business came down to London, and to a shop in Little Tower Street in 1815. Little Tower Street may have disappeared, but H. Sotheran and Son went on from success to bookshops at 140 Strand, and 36 Piccadilly. The Strand shop was closed on the death of Mr. Henry Cecil Sotheran in 1928. Their even longer run in Piccadilly had seen them at three different numbers there; 36, 37, and then at 43, which was the shop that I remember.

The window at No. 43 was pure Piccadilly period, often with a display of some of John Gould's magnificent coloured bird books since the firm had bought the copyright, and the entire stock of these works. But always there was something of Charles Dickens, for Mr. John Harrison Stonehouse, the managing director, was a devotee. This devotion may have been prompted by the memory of the firm's purchase of Dickens's library at Gad's Hill Place in the last century, anyway there were always little pink-taped bundles of some First Editions in the original monthly parts flanked by runs of *The Dickensian*, a periodical which had been started in 1904. It was the most nostalgic shop window in Piccadilly, *pace* Hatchard's almost opposite.

But of all the Sotheran publications and phases the most re-membered is likely to be that of Dr. Heinrich Zeitlinger, and the publication in 1921 of his *Bibliotheca Chemica-Mathematica, a Catalogue of Works in many Tongues on exact and applied Science, with a Subject Index*. In the preface, Dr. Zeitlinger writes that the compiling has taken fifteen years, and 'That it is the first historical catalogue of science published in any country as giving at one, the current price of each book included, bibliographical particulars and many biographical and historical references, both in the descriptions themselves and in the notes.' Today with the three Supplements added to the two original volumes, and which Dr. Zeitlinger worked on up to his death in 1960, this catalogue is still the founding work of reference for all collections in the sciences.

Sotheran's will always remain an essential house of reference for general bibliography in Great Britain during the past two hundred years, because of the many great libraries and collections that passed through their hands and appeared in their catalogues.

First there was Laurence Sterne's library, bought by the firm when still in York. The second great literary purchase was the Charles Dickens library from Gad's Hill Place, the subject of two catalogues. Then came Bishop Gott's splendid library (catalogued as *Bibliotheca Pretiosa*). The Halliwell-Phillips library, and the Warwick Castle Shakespeare Collection were both secured by Sotheran's for the Folger Shakespeare Library, Washington, D.C., with many other Shakespeare quartos and folios to follow.

The two most important transactions during the last century were when Mrs. Rylands entrusted the firm with the purchase of the Althorp Library from Earl Spencer (catalogued by T. F. Dibdin under the title of *Bibliotheca Spenceriana*), and shortly afterwards the purchase of the Earl of Crawford's collection of manuscripts. These two great collections formed the nucleus of the John Rylands Library at Manchester, today the fourth most important library in the country, with the prospect of shortly being appointed as one of the copyright libraries.

Most interesting, however, of all the Henry Sotheran transactions was the negotiation with the Pilgrim Trust, and the sale to them for presentation to Trinity College, Cambridge, of Sir Isaac Newton's library. At the time of the sale they issued a six-page brochure: *The Newton Library, for Sale by Henry Sotheran, Limited, Booksellers to H.M. the King*. Knowing the strange Emmington/Chinnor association with Sir Isaac Newton's library, they have kindly allowed me to quote from the brochure—'The existence of Newton's Library was quite unknown until recent years. Neither Brewster nor the Catalogues of the Portsmouth Collection refer to it, and all other authorities on Newton are equally silent on the question.'

But with the brilliant detective work of Lt.-Col. de Villamil in the early twenties, we now know that from Newton's death in 1717, until 1778, his library was housed intact in the rectory at

Chinnor. The full story of how the Newton library came to Chinnor, and where it went after the death of Dr. Charles Musgrave, the rector, comes at the end of these *Recollections* in the 'Emmington, Chinnor, Oxford' conclusion. In the brochure Sotheran's offered *en bloc*: '... this collection consisting altogether of 858 volumes, nearly all in contemporary calf binding, and with a few exceptions, in excellent preservation. Eighty-three of the books show actual marks of Newton's handwriting, of which twenty have his autograph signature. . . . The great majority of the books have the corners turned down in the peculiar manner practised by Newton, the points always indicating a passage in which he was specially interested. It will thus be possible to trace back some of Newton's thoughts to their very sources. . . . By far the most important items of this collection are the first and second editions of the *Principia*. They are full of corrections, cancellations and additions, all in Newton's handwriting. These corrected copies formed the basis of the new editions, and that of the first edition was actually meant at one time as the copy destined for the printers, for Newton had thoroughly revised the title. These copies have, however, an interest far beyond that of the basis of the second and third editions, for they contain a very large number of additions and alterations which had never been adopted. These corrections thus represent the original thoughts of Newton on first revising the work, and may yet form the starting point of important historical investigations. Indeed, it is not too much to say that the discovery of these copies forms the most important bibliographical find in the domain of science that has been made for very many years.'

Sotheran's have also allowed me to reproduce from their brochure the facsimile of the title-page of the *Principia*.

Just before my time in the book trade, Maggs Bros. had moved (1918) from 109 Strand to 34–35 Conduit Street, and then just before the last war began, made the most aristocratic of all booksellers' moves, to the handsome house in Berkeley Square. Today Maggs Bros. must mean to many booksellers, as it still means to me, the late Mr. Frank Maggs, or just 'Frank' as he was

PHILOSOPHIÆ
NATURALIS
PRINCIPIA
MATHEMATICA.

Autore *JS. NEWTON,* *Trin.* *Coll. Cantab. Soc.* Matheseos
Professore *Lucasiano,* & Societatis Regalis Sodali.

IMPRIMATUR.
S. PEPYS, *Reg. Soc.* PRÆSES.
Julii 5. 1686.

LONDINI,

Jussu *Societatis Regiæ* ac Typis *Josephi Streater.* Prostat apud
plures Bibliopolas. *Anno* MDCLXXXVII.

The title-page prepared for press by Sir Isaac Newton,
but not adopted in the second edition.

affectionately called by many who should not, but inevitably did. He had come down to Cecil Court with one of my early catalogues in which he had 'ticked' many of the travel items. When I wondered about so many ten- and fifteen-shilling items which he was having sent up to Conduit Street, he told me how these little 'inconsiderables' gave him as much pleasure as any prestigious Sothebyana, because he knew what they would mean to his collectors. I am still grateful for this counsel, and for the friendship of one of the best and most unassuming booksellers I have known.

Messrs. J. and E. Bumpus (By Appointment to the King) were at 350 Oxford Street in the twenties and thirties, with canny Mr. Wilson in charge, and the beautiful Court Room for many fine exhibitions. The dignified stores of Marshall and Snelgrove suited them as a neighbour, and it was sad when they moved up the street to No. 477 to face Gordon Selfridge. Sadder still, the last move to Baker Street, almost as if for a last despairing consultation with Sherlock Holmes.

In the twenties and thirties, Pickering and Chatto were in the handsome shop in King Street, St. James's, but I never called there, probably overawed by the praise from that most refined of collectors, the late Richard Jennings, and from the Master himself, the late Michael Sadleir. My friend among the Massey brothers was Gerald, who had a bookshop in Shepherd's Market, still in the thirties the Michael Arlen village. Two Kerry blues sat in the corner of the shop, barking their owner's fame today as bibliographical number one in the dog world. From the Shepherd's Market, Gerald moved to Dog Kennel Hill, in south London, surely the happiest of all booksellers' addresses. Even though he has now moved to Streatham, I still try and keep him posted with any printing of the hair of any dog.

In *Minding My Own Business* (Chatto and Windus, 1956), Mr. Percy Muir gracefully records the intricate comings and goings of the firm of Elkin Mathews. I only remember the first floor at 78 Grosvenor Street, with the different directors all in depressed hauteur, but this was the phase which Percy describes as 'the gloom of Grosvenor Street'. Today one is much more at home with the old firm's offshoot 'Deval and Muir', with regular visits from Laurie Deval, and with the occasional one from Percy. The catalogues too from Takeley, Hertfordshire, in which the learning sits as easily as the modesty of the pricing. Amongst other comings and goings, the one aptly and economically recorded is in the advertisement 'The Rarest Books, the Finest Manuscripts. William H. Robinson, Ltd., 16 & 17 Pall Mall, London S.W.1'.

Of the final goings during these years, the loss of Marks & Co. two years ago, may still reverberate down the Charing Cross Road, but that of Ellis echoes not only down Bond Street, but down two hundred years. Ellis's was the oldest bookshop in London, with its history written by the two last partners in 1928, and its epitaph in the names of its customers: Dr. Johnson, Mrs. Piozzi, William Beckford, Lord Ashburnham, the Earl of Crawfurd, Robert Hoe, and Henry Huth. Aesthetically too, a loss with the shop front, one of the finest eighteenth-century shop façades in London.

In a collective 'Vale' to the old Brigade of Brigands, there are special memories of old Ben Bailey of Newington Butts, and his two pals from Clapham, Harry Gallup of the Pavement, and Preston & Co.; Harry Davey from the Minories, Eustace Tallboys from Islington Green, Messrs. Jeffreys and Davidson with their string of barrows in the Farringdon Road. A breed not likely to be seen again. They wore bowlers, cloth caps, and chokers. They disdained bibliographies and the consulting of *Book Auction Records*; a title-page and a good memory were sufficient for their pricing. They were shrewd enough, but not greedy.

Old Ben Bailey was almost a legend when I first met and talked to him at his last country sale. He looked like the Salvation Army's General Booth, though without the General's menacing nose, and his shop was along from Spurgeon's Tabernacle at 62 Newington Butts, SE11. By the time I got down to the shop, the old man was bedridden, and the two sons were in charge. Their speciality was a 'Betting Book', and they spent most of the afternoon dashing out for the papers with the racing results. I was only allowed to go up to the first floor, because they said that the floors of the upper rooms and the staircase were rotten. A few years ago, my old friend, Mr. Brereton of Marlow, told me that when a young man living in South London, he too had come to 62 Newington Butts and had not been allowed to go further up than the first floor. However, he had drawn up and signed a statement, absolving the Bailey sons from all blame if he fell through the floor, and they let him go all the way up. From these top rooms, he remembers three illuminated manuscripts so soggy that it took weeks to dry them out, black-letter folios that had to be left where the mice had nibbled too many of the margins, and incunables that were brought down in any condition. And coming down, one or other of the brothers might edge up, slip an early printed volume from his pocket with a muttered 'Ten bob governor, but don't let 'im know'.

Of the shops of this period which one did not know, and now wishes one had: Everard Meynell's 'The Serendipity Shop' in East Chapel Street, W1, with his catalogue No. 4, 1920, including the library of Coventry Patmore, many of his manuscripts, autograph letters from Carlyle, Tennyson, Leigh Hunt, Francis Thompson, and Thomas Hardy. More exquisite still, Christopher Millard at the Bungalow, 8 Abercorn Place, when 'Bungalow' was chic, and quite suitable for the Beardsley and Wilde he specialized in. His catalogue No. 6, 1921, lists an original caricature of Whistler by Beardsley, £110; an original cartoon of the Wildes, by Max Beerbohm, £25; and an oil painting of Oscar Wilde, by Harper Pennington, £200. Harold Edwards is the only person I know to have visited the Bungalow, and he says that it is as well that I didn't.

Some London Booksellers

However important their bookshops, there are always the book-sellers who seem more important than their shops, and among these, the late E. P. Goldschmidt comes first. From the outset he specialized in manuscripts, early printed and sixteenth-century books and bookbindings. Books of hours and illuminated manuscripts were never of so much interest to him as texts; like the humanists of the Renaissance he was concerned with the transmission of texts. These were the contents of the series of catalogues which he was to issue during his thirty-one years as a bookseller, and which ended with *Catalogue One Hundred* just before his death in 1954. This was no ordinary catalogue, every book in it had already been sold! It contained the descriptions of one hundred books and manuscripts which had been sold direct to private customers and libraries without ever being offered for sale in any of the catalogues that were current at the time of their acquisition. More and more these catalogues will become an indispensable source of reference; an incomplete set recently sold for several hundreds of pounds in the auction room. That my own set has so many gaps is unforgivable because the co-compiler is my oldest friend in the book trade. Robert Dougan and I studied together for the London University diplomas in librarianship. When I went on to Hodgson's, he went to become E. P. Goldschmidt's first assistant, staying with him till his call-up in 1941. Demobilized, Robert Dougan, in love with Scotland where he had been stationed, and not fancying a return to London, became librarian of the Sandeman Library in Perth. From Perth he went on to Dublin as librarian at Trinity College, and today is librarian of the Henry E. Huntington Library and Art Gallery at San Marino, California.

Besides these hundred catalogues, E.P.G. left behind thirty-two books, papers, and articles on the bibliography of the period in which he was the master. It is by two of these, *Gothic and Renaissance Bookbindings*, published in 1928, and *The Printed Book of the Renaissance*, also printed by the Cambridge University Press in 1950, that he will be most remembered. By contrast, my memories may be ephemeral, but I hope they may add to the picture of a great man.

E.P.G. used to love walking around London when it had returned to its quiet dark self after the war, and we would meet when he came round the British Museum, beside which was my flat. I would go back with him to the old Brown's Hotel where he dined each evening, and then back to 45 Old Bond Street for coffee and his stories. He was born in Vienna in 1887, and went up to Trinity College, Cambridge, in 1905. During his four years at Cambridge the evidence of his early love of old books, manuscripts, and bookbindings is in the privately printed and annotated catalogue of seventy-five of his best books for presentation to his friends, amongst whom were Rupert Brooke, Sir Stephen Gaselee, and Lord Keynes. It was Cambridge with the memories, and still with the presences of the most famous of all modern academic generations: G. E. Moore, Bertrand Russell, Lytton Strachey, E. M. Forster, and the Keynes brothers, and it was these years that probably gave E.P.G. his lifelong affection for England. After Cambridge he went back to Vienna and until his war-work with the Dutch Red Cross (with a Dutch father, he never gave up his Dutch nationality), he was able to continue with his hobby, visiting the Austrian monastic libraries, and checking thousands of incunabula for the projected *Gesamtkatalog der Wiegendrucke*. At the same time, he developed his interest in medieval text manuscripts by studying and describing those he found in these libraries. With the post-war German inflation cutting badly into his personal fortune, he came back to England and started an antiquarian book business. He arrived in London in 1923, with a small but first-class reference library, his collection of old bookbindings, a few other books and manuscripts, and he was to be blessed with the most suitable premises. Laurence Sterne's old house at 45 Old Bond Street was for renting. E.P.G. had only brought a small capital with him, but knew at once that Sterne's gently freakish ghost was for him, and it remained so for the rest of his life.

Not surprisingly, his favourite book among the moderns was André Gide's *Paludes*. Somewhat surprising was the discovery that he was writing a study of Britain's trading and banking role in the world and its future development when the war was over. It was published pseudonymously in 1942 by Macmillan as *England's Service*, by 'Sarpedon', who, it will be remembered, was the result of the union of Europa with the bull. Always deploring petty nationalities, there is the added interest today of E. P. Goldschmidt combining the good European with the best of John Bull. One of my last memories is of him reading from a letter he had just received from a clever new assistant of whom he had great hopes. Jacques Vellekoop was writing from Paris, but what pleased E.P.G. was nothing to do with the finding of books, just that the young man was enjoying himself so much. While *The Times*, in its obituary, described the late 'E. Ph. Goldschmidt' as 'the most learned member of the international antiquarian book-trade', he was also a very all-round humanist.

After the Goldschmidt caviare, the London course of Andrew Block. No two booksellers could be more different, but they appreciated each other, were great friends, and used to meet on most Saturday afternoons at the Express Dairy tea rooms in New Oxford Street. They were the founding members of a modest little tea party of some of the most knowledgeable bookmen in London, with F. S. Ferguson, R. A. Peddie, and H. W. Davies as the most regular members, and among the visitors, Dr. John Johnson, and Bill Jackson of Harvard.

Opening his first bookshop in West Hampstead in 1911, Andrew Block must be the living father to the English book trade. By cautious stages from West Hampstead, he arrived in the West End (Dean Street) in 1929, and it was there that I first met him. It was a small shop, because he was torn between writing and selling books. In 1926, with the late Charlie Stonehill, he had compiled the four-volume *Anonyma and Pseudonyma*, still a useful complement to Halkett and Laing's *Dictionary of Anonymous and Pseudonymous English Literature*, but today difficult to find. There were other publications during his four years in Dean Street, *The Book Collector's Vade-mecum* (1932), the *Short History of the Booksellers* (1933), and the *Sir James Barrie Bibliography*. In 1933, he moved to Bloomsbury Court, near Holborn, where he stayed for the next twenty-five years, then round the corner into Barter Street, where at 82, he still bobs about, as cheery and active as I remember forty years earlier. Bloomsbury Court suited him perfectly, with a deceptively little shop on the ground floor, and a twisting staircase leading down to a great cavern with Andrew in a corner surrounded by pin-ups of his favourite customers and film stars. It was there that I bought one of Claude Lovat Fraser's most decorative drawings, the costume design for Brummell in the production of Blanche Jerrold's *Beau Brummell*, signed and dated '20 Nov. 1920'. It hangs here between two signed proofs of Gordon Craig's designs for *Hamlet*, also from Andrew, an especially happy buy since the great man's son Edward Craig, who lives three miles away from here under the Chilterns, is a very old and good friend of us both. A few years ago, a visitor stopped in front of the Beau Brummell with a wail of 'Andrew?' He had seen the drawing in the basement in Bloomsbury Court, hesitated, slept on it, and gone round next day to be told, 'Sorry old boy'. He still remembered it as one of the misses he misses most.

Today, Barter Street, with a large shop, and two caverns downstairs, still cannot contain Andrew's buying. The mountains of folders labelled 'Playbills' and 'Theatrical Prints' show his first loves, the theatre, the music-hall, and the cinema. Start him on one of these, and it will be a torrent; the great theatrical libraries he has bought, the special treasures which are downstairs although he can't remember where, and the actors, stars, and starlets who have called. Even if most of them are in partial to complete eclipse, they still shine for Andrew. But one of his last assignments does look like lasting, i.e., his furnishing of the library at Disneyland with its miniature books! For literature, he recalls as customers and friends: Aleister Crowley, John Galsworthy, D. H., and T. E. Lawrence, Bernard Shaw (Andrew had founded, and was first chairman of the Shaw Society), Hugh Walpole, and T. J. Wise, whom most charitably he remembers as affable. But Andrew isn't mesmerized by his gentle ghosts. From his theatre folk he learned that the show must go on, so when the door of the shop opens, Andrew forgets his story, and almost leaps to serve. It makes no difference to him that today it is long-haired, shaggy, and sex indeterminate, they too are as serious about books and prints as the old, trim, immaculate. Andrew Block is the ageless bookseller.

After the Goldschmidt caviare and Bloomsbury's Andrew Block, comes Walworth's Fred Bason. In the four volumes of his *Diary* with the prefaces by Nicholas Bentley, L. A. G. Strong, and Sir Noel Coward, he asks to be known as 'the Cockney book-barrow boy', and cock sparrow suits him.

Fred appeared in Cecil Court soon after I opened. He was on his way home after the Tuesday morning hunt in the old Caledonian Market. There wasn't much I fancied in his sack, but he brought along suggestions. Did I know about the wonderful pickings at the series of Christmas jumble sales which were now starting? I didn't. Fred then would buy another ticket for the St. George's Hospital Jumble next week, and I would meet him at Hyde Park Corner at 1.30 for the early door. Success meant being at the head of the queue, and we lined up along the hospital wall, mainly determined-looking women, and a few men in cloth caps each, like Fred, with a sack. Looking at the bus stop opposite, I was rather glad that I had not brought a sack. Happier too when the door was opened, and no-one I knew had got on or got off a No. 72 bus. Fred had briefed me in the technique, which was to rush to the book-stall, ignore what was set out, and dive through the draperies to see what the indignant stall-holders were hiding for their special pals. I'm glad that I went to one Christmas jumble.

Fred was to go on with helpful suggestions, i.e. there was

Southend-on-Sea, with a dozen bookshops full of good books. We motored down to Southend one February morning and could not find one bookshop, so we walked out to the Kursaal and picknicked in a shelter surrounded by frozen mud. A visit to a country house near Banbury just avoided another disaster. Fred had the introduction through one of his swell pals. The lady was gracious and explained that Blackwell's of Oxford had been yesterday, and she had arranged for two other London booksellers to come down the following week. Fred said that he didn't care. He didn't want that sort of book, novels were his kind, the love stories the servants read. They went down to the servants' quarters and up the stairs came the wrangle 'ninepence is my price, not a penny more; what d'ye fink we've come all this way for?' Fred was winning, so I got out half a dozen books from the shelves and when he came up with his armful of novels I said, 'We've got to get these for ten quid.' I did not enjoy hovering in a corner during this second battle, but Fred enjoyed it, and won, and the day was saved. There was another bonus to that expedition. On the way home we stopped in Aylesbury and I met again Mr. Frank Weatherhead whom I had last seen before the war in his bookshop in George Lane, Folkestone. When Folkestone was evacuated at the beginning of the war, Mr. Weatherhead came back to his native Aylesbury, opening his bookshop in the town square. Today it is still there, three times the size, run by young Frank and his son Nick, with one of the fourth generation showing an interest in books. It's good to know that there is this future for one of the best bookshops inside the forty-mile radius round London.

I'm glad that I was able to make some sort of return for Fred's many suggestions. One afternoon when Fred was with me at the back of the shop, a lady came in to say that she was leaving her flat in the Charing Cross Road, and there were a number of books I might like to buy. I recognized her from a signed photograph in the window of Mr. Freed's ballet shoe shop at the end of Cecil Court. She was peeping over a large ostrich fan, with nothing much else on except Mr. Freed's shoes. I didn't think her books would be mine, introduced Fred, and off they went. An hour

later Fred came back with a bundle of novels, also opening his
attaché case to show me four of the lady's vests. His mother ran an
old clothes stall, so on her behalf, Fred had asked if the lady had
any clothes for sale. He had been shown some dance frocks (the
lady danced in the cabaret at Grosvenor House), but Fred had
reckoned that these were too flash for the tarts down his way, so
he made do with these vests at fourpence each, and arranged that
his mother would call during that week. Later, the dancer came in
to ask about Fred. After business was over, Fred had asked her
about Grosvenor House, suggested that she was rather stout, and
could she really manage her steps? Before she knew, Fred was at
the piano, and she was being put through high kicks.

The piano was one of his sidelines. On Saturday afternoon he
played non-stop in a furniture shop. When I wrote to ask him
more about this sideline, he replied, 'Certainly, I played a piano
in a Bermondsey shop, but only because they sold secondhand
pianos, and it was my job to make them sound well. No-one else
in the shop could play, and my music made people stop, and come
in, and buy pianos between £6 and £10 a time. I was paid 10s.
to play from 2 till 6 almost non-stop. I'd stop only to show people
the insides of the piano, and for sales talk. If I sold a piano I got
2s. 6d. commission. It was ever so helpful, also it enabled me to
practise, and fill a Saturday afternoon, and I met people, and
offered to teach them the piano. (I had two lessons at 1s. 6d. each
from a Miss Smith when I was 15, and did not even have a piano.)
In 5 years, I taught 18 people to play the piano at 1s. for an hour's
lesson. I only had one failure; a lady of 63 who just could not be
taught. I had to earn money for a desperate reason. My mother
wanted me to be a barber. She said, "Pay me 30s. a week, and you
can be a bookman for as long as you can pay me 30s. a week. But
the week you fail to pay me 30s. you stop bookselling and stop
writing, and go back to the barber's shop." At times I was desperate for that 30s., which when I was 16 was a great deal of money.
Hence I did many things I would not have done otherwise. But
from the age of 16 till now at 64, it has always been Books. I am
wedded to Books. My life devoted to them, and lived every year.

No regrets.' When I sent Fred his story for approval, and any corrections, he sent back two, 'My mother had her clothes stall in Brixton, and I had my bookstall in Bermondsey, never ever in Walworth. We do not pee on our own doorstep.'

Today I am still glad to be receiving Fred's lists of 'Real Good Books for Sale', but it will be by his own books that he will be remembered. The four *Diaries*, and the Bibliography of his old friend Somerset Maugham. During the early twenties when Maugham had four comedies running concurrently in the West End, Fred had written suggesting an improvement here and there. Maugham went down to have tea with the family in Walworth, and there is a snapshot of him sitting on the dustbin at the back door. Surely a vital exhibit in any William Somerset Maugham iconography—the happy perch on a Walworth dustbin alongside Graham Sutherland's brilliantly tortured mandarin, and the insouciance of Sir Gerald Kelly? There is also *The Saturday Book*, to which Fred has been the most consistent of all the contributors, with an article in every number from five to thirty. The B.B.C. archives have his thirty talks in *Woman's Hour*, and there was one television appearance too. This was about 1949 at Alexandra Palace; he was a little nervous and I went along in support. The late Richard Dimbleby was in charge, but the set and programme he had arranged wasn't for long. Fred had a parcel of prints, drawing pins, string, and a bottle of paste. The kind Mr. Dimbleby couldn't both laugh and protest, and Fred had his way, even with the word 'customers' which was how he described the audience and his viewers. And if most of these activities are now over, he is still ready to lecture to Rotary Clubs and Evergreens anywhere in England. The Walworth Council have just moved him from his old home in Westmoreland Road into one of their new flats. His new address is 'Mr. F. T. Bason, 4 Broadmayne, Portland Street, London, SE17'.

If Fred Bason was the London urchin who somehow made good, my fourth bookseller, the late Bertram Rota, was the pedigree bookseller of that period. The bookseller who, in spite of the pedigree and the lustre he was to add to it, always found time for

Fred. Today, Fred remembers Bertram Rota as his most sympathetic benefactor in the trade. The grandson of the great bookseller-publisher Bertram Dobell, he started his apprenticeship to
the trade in 1918 in the Charing Cross Road bookshop of his uncle
Percy, and Arthur Dobell. In 1923, aged 19, and with £100
borrowed from his mother, he started on his own business in a
couple of upstair rooms at 108 Charing Cross Road. In 1927, he
moved to Davies Street, W1, where I first met him, and where
he stayed until 1934. After that, there were three years in Old
Burlington Street, and a move in 1937 to Vigo Street and John
Lane's old Bodley Head, or Bodley House, as it was then called.
He was there till 1965, in the building which, with the grace of its
eighteenth-century architecture and its literary traditions of the
Nineties, so suited his personality. He was joined there in 1952 by
his son Anthony, and the added young thrust inevitably showed
these premises to be too confining. In June 1965, came the move
to the present grand shop at 4, 5, and 6 Saville Row, W1.

From the beginning, modern first editions and manuscripts
were Bertram Rota's main interest. In the end, his name became
synonymous with these all over the world. Even if this was no
common meeting ground for us, we were always running into
each other through common customers, and the geography of
London and the sale rooms in the kindest of trade ways. There
was also our mutual care for the affairs of Fred Bason. Somerset
Maugham first editions were laid aside so that Fred could have
the first option. Fred, in turn, would lay them aside until he had
word from Maugham that he would be at the Dorchester on a
certain afternoon. Fred then took along these first editions, each
with a slip having the name of a collector, usually American, who
wanted his copy inscribed and signed by Maugham himself.
Maugham obliged with heartfelt and 'unmaugham'-like messages,
with one stipulation that the profit in the little game was to be
divided between Fred and St. Thomas's Hospital.

In my notes and memories of Fred Bason, his *Apologia pro sua
Vita et Libris* stands in the letter he sent me, and which he has
given me permission to quote. Now, with Anthony Rota's per-

mission, I quote from the brief account which he found in his father's handwriting, after his death in 1966. It was dated 1964, and ended, 'This is the record of a happy life amongst books, rich in interest and in daily discoveries, made entrancing by friendships amongst colleagues at home and abroad and made contented at the end by the assurance that the tradition will continue through another generation, and perhaps a third. After that, who knows? But books go on.' Today, it is good to think that the bookseller who was too modest to get office in the Antiquarian Booksellers' Association, of which he was such a loyal member, would have been so happy seeing his son Anthony as this year's President.

Mr. Charles Salkeld was the most complete of all the London booksellers. He was born over his father's bookshop in Red Lion Court in the late 1880s, lived behind his shop in Clapham Road, south London, until it was blitzed in the early part of the war, and died over his bookshop in Dulwich Village. His father had the reputation for an unusual stock which he drew, not from the London sale rooms, but from the little bookshops and corners he called on all over England. Mr. Gladstone was one of his customers, and our Mr. Salkeld loved telling the story of one of these Gladstone visits, when his father's tame jackdaw, who had the flight of the shop, alighted on the brim of Mr. Gladstone's top hat. The family waited uneasily, but the worst did not happen. I call him 'our Mr. Salkeld', because going down to see how things were after the bomb, I suggested that he might fill in the time by coming to help us in Cecil Court. We liked having him there, and we thought that he was happy too. It was only later one realized that it had been the caging of a wild duck. He loved roaming the book corners of the country which he had got to know from his father. There he picked up the oddments which gave his little catalogues their character, with 'Charming' and 'Curious' the rather overworked adjectives. I still remember 'A charming little wash drawing of two charming ladies standing in the corner of a charming little field'. 'Curious' for him meant only the odder Valentine or old Christmas card, a Broadsheet of an execution scene, or a coarse Election Address. 'Sex' wasn't at all curious for Mr. Salkeld.

Happily the governors of Dulwich College were to release him from the Cecil Court cage. They leased him one of their 'charming' cottages in the old village, and although there were restrictions, he was allowed to carry on his trade, discreetly. A few old prints and books in the parlour window were all that was necessary; he and 'Mother', as he always spoke of Mrs. Salkeld, soon had all their old customers and friends round them again. Theirs was the happiest of book trade partnerships, with 'Mother' putting in her little spoke, and Mr. Salkeld patiently waiting till she had finished her 'would you believe it'.

Mr. Francis Norman, like Charlie Salkeld, lived with and among his books. In his first shop in Windmill Street, just off the Tottenham Court Road, he and Mrs. Norman lived behind the shop. When they moved round the corner into one of the pretty little row of late eighteenth-century houses in Whitfield Street, it was above the shop. When Whitfield Street was destroyed by a flying bomb at the end of the war, it was to Heath Street, Hampstead, where Francis Norman still happily lives above his shop. In the books these two dealt in, they were alike only in the books that left them cold, the standard work which could be always found somewhere in the end, the handsomely bound library set, or the very expensive Sotheby hall-marked item.

I first met Francis Norman viewing the stacks in the basement at Hodgson's in 1930. He and Mrs. Norman had not been long in their little antique shop in Windmill Street, when they found that the few books about the shop sold better than the antiques. Discovering Hodgson's, and the lots of stacks with which the sales always ended, he would spend a morning going through these stacks, marking his catalogue, picking out a volume and reading extracts from it to Jim or one of the other porters who only thought it rather sad, and said among themselves 'crackers'.

A year after the discovery of Hodgson's, there wasn't room for the books in Windmill Street, the antiques were dropped, and the Normans moved into their real bookshop in Whitfield Street. There, and for the next fifteen years, Francis Norman carried on as the answer to the prayer of the discriminating and sometimes penniless academics of London and America. Amongst the Americans, the staunchest was Professor T. W. Baldwin of Illinois University. When his classic two volumes on the school books of the Elizabethans appeared, *Small Latin and Less Greek*, the preface gave grateful acknowledgement to the help of two booksellers. Inevitably the late Mr. F. S. Fergusson of the House of Quaritch, and Mr. Francis Norman.

Among his quiet English academics, Professor Beale of the London School of Economics, and the late Dr. Saxl of the Warburg Institute, are witnesses to the width of Norman's stock. Among the noisier there was the late Harold Laski with his sensational story of the book bargain he had just picked up. No-one ever believed these stories, and every one was astounded, even Laski himself; they were just part of the cheerfulness which he brought along to the bookshops, the lecture rooms at the London School of Economics, even to General Elections.

Early in the war, some of Norman's London friends thought that they would like to say thank you for so much pleasure and profit during years that never looked like coming round again. The late Dr. Saxl did the organizing and then came to me with the cheque which he thought might come easier from an old trade friend. It was pleasant to say to a fellow bookseller 'What luck to be in a trade where this sort of thing can happen.'

A few weeks after this paragraph, I met Francis Norman at Sotheby's and told him what I was doing. He was amused, but wondered if any of our contemporaries were worth writing about, which made me wonder too! Still the book was going to be more after the style of Charles Knight's *Shadows of the Old Booksellers* (1867), than Dr. Rosenbach's *Books and Bidders* (1927), and it may be that when paperbacks, offset reprints, and the computers have finally taken over, the twenty-first century will be glad to have these last shades of my old booksellers, however shadowy.

The fifth and last London bookseller in my period, was unique in being first collector, then bookseller, and finally bookseller's assistant. This may sound like a descent and a sad story, actually little Evans was perfectly happy in each of his three stages, probably happiest in the last. I never knew his initials, or Christian name, it was always 'little Evans'. In Mr. Percy Muir's *Minding My Own Business*, there is a photograph of the great bookman, A. W. Evans, showing a volume to little Evans, but the description only states 'A. W. Evans (right) in his room at 33 Conduit Street'—little Evans, private as ever, and as he liked to be.

I first met him as the collector of sixteenth- and seventeenth-century English literature and heavy buyer at Hodgson's. He was badly hit by the collapse on Wall Street and decided to become a bookseller. His shop was, like Norman's, in Windmill Street, but had no character at all. What seemed to be a catastrophic change in his style of book almost seemed to amuse little Evans. If there were more puffings at the cigarettes, there were even more gentle smiles. The bookshop lasted hardly a year, and for the next fifteen years he went to help one friend after another in their bookshops. Privately, one added 'Jonah' to the 'little', because invariably minor disasters came to these friends. The reason had nothing to do with little Evans, merely that his good friends were usually too good even for the undemanding rigours of the book trade. There was, however, one major disaster during these helping years. His old friend the late Leslie Chaundy had asked him to help in the bookshop in Dover Street. One Saturday morning little Evans had not gone in, and a flying bomb made a direct hit, killing Mr. Chaundy and the rest of the staff.

After the war came a late but very happy marriage. and with Mrs. Evans having a cottage near Hitchin, it looked like the perfect finale; little Evans quietly enjoying Hertfordshire as his favourite author, Charles Lamb, had done on his retirement. But booksellers, especially the humble ones, are spared from retirement. The West End book scrabble called in a way that the East India House didn't. There was a sensible compromise. During the week he lived in a room full of books in Victoria, and at the weekends in Hertfordshire, both Charles Lamb and little Evans living happily ever after.

A London Street Market

The Rosens' bookstall was in Rupert Street, leading off Shaftesbury Avenue, and a few minutes walk from Piccadilly Circus.
Mr. Rosen, fat and short, was a master tailor with business
premises in the family flat round the corner. When the 'Fifty
Shilling Tailors' became a threat, Mr. Rosen was really rather glad,
the street market on his doorstep had always fascinated him, and
as there was a stall for everything except books, he decided to sell
books. The most ill-suited bookseller of all time, he had not only
never read a book, but most of the time, hated them. When
business was bad, he used to walk around the basement where the
books were stored overnight, kicking the poor bundles, and mut-
tering 'Bleedin' things!' This basement was across the pavement
from the stall. He had the front room, and a couple of Poles with
a flower stall had the back. Mrs. Rosen spent most of the day in
the basement; she was bored at home, and here she had a stove to
make tea, and entertain her husband's customers and her Soho
friends. There were always a lot of symptoms during Mrs. Rosen's
entertaining, and Mr. Rosen took her and their two boys to
Margate for a week to see if the sea air made any difference. They
all hated it, and were back before their week ended. The boys
were chubby and sensible; when the elder became a bus conductor
because of the prospects, his father was disgusted. The most important person in the Rosen project was 'Dirty Ernie', family
friend, bibliographical adviser, seeker after fresh stock (mainly the
throw-outs from friendly booksellers), their man from Reuter's,
who trotted round the bookshops telling them when their sort of
book had arrived on the stall.

One evening when Ernie appeared in Cecil Court, it was not with the usual 'Come at once' but to ask me if I would come to Rupert Street next morning at 11.30. A lovely library had come their way, but had not yet been bought. Mr. Rosen had still to make an offer, and was, for once, nervous. Would I go along and help? Next morning, Mr. Rosen was extra Soho smart, the family excited, only Ernie looked doubtful. I became doubtful when the taxi put us down in Albemarle Street and at the doors of the Royal Institution of Great Britain. But the porter knew of the appointment, and while we waited for the President in the beautiful library, Mr. Rosen explained. The President's cook bought her vegetables in the market, had chummed up with Mrs. Rosen and, grateful for the entertaining in the basement, had promised to ask her missis if the President had any old books going. Apparently he had, and that is why we were there. The President was very kind, and almost understood, even if I did not know cook's name. The books were library duplicates, mainly odd runs of foreign scientific periodicals, valuable I'm sure, but as I told the President, really for a firm that specialized in periodicals and could make a proper offer. All this had to be very delicately done, not for the President's feelings, but because Mr. Rosen was walking about the library looking moody, and likely to kick the books with the usual 'Bleedin' things!' The visit ended happily; I got out, and Mr. Rosen was taken down to see cook, and the President was sure that he could find him some books for Soho in the flat upstairs.

It was for their introduction to Dirty Ernie, rather than for their books, that I was grateful to *famille* Rosen. Ernie shared a basement flat in Old Compton Street with his brother. The brother was a pavement artist, entertaining pit and gallery theatre queues by tearing up newspapers into portraits of celebrities. At nights, Ernie used to take back volumes from the stall to throw at the rats scuttling round their beds.

Besides the Rosens, Ernie helped out 'Iron-Foot Jack', whom pre-war Londoners will probably remember lecturing, in mortarboard and gown, on a rostrum at street corners around Soho. The iron heel was to help a club foot, and Ernie also helped by carrying the rostrum. The lecture was on astrology. When it was finished, Ernie went round the crowd collecting personal data which he handed to the lecturer. He then handed back the individual prognostications and collected the sixpences. The police were more amused with Iron-Foot Jack's lectures than they were with another of his sidelines, the Green Carnation Club, which he ran for lonely waiters in Greek Street, Soho. It was raided one night, and Iron-Foot Jack was run in along with some of the waiters happily dancing with each other. More happily for Ernie, that night he was not on duty at the cloakroom.

Ernie had once told me about his mother, a dancer at the beginning of the century who had gone to Paris with her troupe when these English dancing troupes became the rage in the French music-halls. The two little boys had been left with their grandmother, and the money came back but never the mother. Ernie still remembered the stage name of the beautiful mother, and one day in a French theatrical periodical I came across that name under a photograph. Next time Ernie came in I handed it to him. Poor old boy, he sat down at the front of the shop, looked at it, and left without a word.

In the last year of the war, he was sitting in a café in Drury Lane when a flying bomb hit the shop next door, and Ernie's skull was crushed by the marble top of one of the tables hurled across the café. He was taken to a hospital in Reading where they did their best, but he was only able to stagger around with two sticks. He managed to get across streets and visit us in Cecil Court, but the visits became less, and then stopped.

Hodgson's Sale Room

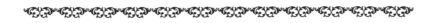

I went to Hodgson's in 1926, replying to their advertisement for a cataloguer in the *Times Literary Supplement*. In those days, applications were in handwriting, and the Hodgson brothers seeing the script which they had learned at Tonbridge in 1889–90, and I, during the First World War, looked no further. The old boy network may be deplorable, but it does have its charm. Mr. John, the senior partner, had written, and the Oxford University Press just published (1924), *The History of Aeronautics in Great Britain to the Latter Half of the Nineteenth Century*. In Chancery Lane he looked after important books and clients, while Mr. Sidney saw that the three cataloguers got ready the catalogues for the fortnightly sales. His hobby and love was for the Stationers' Company of London. Two years ago, having to wait for a train at Charing Cross station, I went into the tea-room. The table I made for had Mr. Sidney at it, correcting catalogue proofs. He was then 92, and too busy to notice me sit down beside him, and in reply to my 'Still these catalogue proofs, Mr. Sidney?' came his old familiar 'Bless my soul! Well I never!'

The third of the personalities of these days was little Jim, least and greatest of the servants in the firm's history. He had been born in Paradise Row, Lambeth, in 1878, and lived there till his death almost ninety years later. He came to Hodgson's in 1890 at seven shillings a week, and had to be persuaded to retire in 1960. A little hunchback, he looked after the books coming in, but his pleasure was seeing that the coal fires in the basement and on the two floors above were kept stacked. He was a widower, with a family now off his hands, and whom he had almost forgotten. The year after

I came, he married again, a flower girl whose pitch had been in the Strand. Physically as ill-matched, as they were happy in everything else; she was a battered Juno with a broken nose and the hoarse voice and laugh of the all-weather flower gel. There was the nostalgia for the days of the old shawl in the silk scarf which she always wore, draped on her broad shoulders. She knew that she had fascinated the young gentleman who spoke proper like, and she wanted to entertain him with her inexhaustible Lambeth and Strand lore. It must have been hard for her to emasculate and spoil the best of her stories, but, like Eliza Doolittle, she was a woman of natural good taste. Jim's hero was Charlie Chaplin. The families had been neighbours, until the Chaplin boys were left orphans and were taken into the Cuckoo School at Hanwell.

The fourth personality of these years was one of the buyers at the sales, David of Cambridge. Gustave David had been born in France and still spoke with a guttural accent. A stout little man, in a long shabby coat and bowler, he came up from Cambridge for most of the sales, spending an uninhibited night or two at the old Shaftesbury Hotel. He had his own place under the rostrum, and sat through the sales munching buns from the pockets of the old coat. He bought grandly and eclectically, and it was always left to his devoted Jim to box up the books in tea chests and send them down to the famous bookstall on Peas Hill in Cambridge. There, the undergraduate collectors of the future were waiting to help him unpack—the Keyneses, Lord Rothschild, and C. K. Ogden. Gustave David is the only Cambridge tradesman to have been given a celebratory dinner in King's College by his devoted customers. Hanging in the study here is the broadside printed in his honour in the thirties. At the head, a woodcut of the old man in the overcoat and bowler, hunched up alongside the piled-up stall, with the folios on the ground beside him. Underneath, a sonnet starting with the line 'Eight lustra now have hastened to their close', and ending, 'Ghost feet shall find one bookstall on the Stygian shore.'

The stall was not able to cope with the cascade of books from

Hodgson's and from Sotheby's too, so David had two cottages on the north side of the square to take the overflow and the unsaleable. When the City Council requisitioned the cottages, David had a problem, and the late C. K. Ogden the solution; a syndicate who would buy the books blind. These were carried across to Kings, where Ogden and his syndicate picked their fancies, with the final discards taken away to be pulped. Among these discards were a number of calf and morocco gilt sets, and even if they were incomplete, this unusual, tender-hearted syndicate sickened at the thought of them being pulped. C. K. Ogden was there with another mischievous, 'basic English' idea. The sets were packed in tea chests, and sent down at decent intervals to the Revd. Montague Summers, historian of Restoration drama and expert on witchcraft, then living at Brighton. Ogden and his friends saw Monty opening the first chest, lovingly setting out the sets, and a little puzzled by the missing volumes, then brightening with chest number two and on till the last and the awful reality. The story of David's odds, and Ogden's prank came out, when one evening in my shop, he saw rows of handsome but odd volumes, and asking where I had got them, I told him, from a Brighton bookseller. When I said that they were reserved for Lord Beaverbrook, he was delighted that at last David's odd lambs were having such an odd shepherd.

On 17 December 1926, there was the excitement of having been at Hodgson's when Mr. John knocked down to Ben Maggs for £2,100, John Bunyan's *A Book for Boys and Girls*, 1688. This was the highest price so far recorded in the hundred years' history of the firm. Today, there would hardly be a ripple at Sotheby & Co. (Hodgson's Rooms), 115 Chancery Lane. Six months later, Mr. John was knocking down, also to Ben Maggs, an item which gave the poor man a more horrid surprise, a beautiful little copy of Charles Lamb's *King and Queen of Hearts* tied up in a bundle with other juveniles of the period. It had been sent in with some other discards by Sir Sydney Cockerell from the Fitzwilliam Museum. The collection had been handed to me for lotting up and cataloguing, and in only six months' apprenticeship this anonymous trifle meant nothing. For my sake, even for Hodgson's, though

not of course for the Fitzwilliam's, it would have been happier if
it had only been Ben Maggs who had spotted it, but a catalogue
at the end of the room started to wave and wave, and Ben Maggs
went on quietly nodding. As a bundle which Mr. John and the
rest of the room had settled for a few pounds at the most went
into the hundreds, it was snatched from the porter in the pound,
and excited booksellers tried to find what was making the price.
Meanwhile Ben Maggs and the unknown at the end of the room
bid steadily up and up. After so many years, and no doubt the
trauma of the inquest, I have forgotten exactly how many
hundreds Ben Maggs paid for his find.

There could be finds in the bundles on the shelves in the sale
room, but it was the stacks with which every sale in these days
ended and which we built up in the basement, that could be the
real fun. There was one which I am glad that I found in Sotheby's
rather than in Hodgson's basement! It was the stack at the end of
the sale of the library of a British consul at Naples. The consul had
been a great collector and historian of Italian goldware. In the
library, there were hundreds of pamphlets, offprints, and wrap-
pered articles from periodicals on the Italian goldsmiths, and
these had been made up into one stack. I offered them to the
Victoria and Albert Museum as a collection, but they replied that
there would be too much duplicating of their own holdings, but
if I would list and offer separately, they would be grateful. Even in
the thirties one did not think of less than five shillings an item, and
compared with my original offer, the transaction ended satis-
factorily, and there was still the real sweetness of this stack left.
As well as being a great collector, the consul had been very social
and a great snob. On top of the stack there were fifty old photographs, many in their silver frames, of his royal and distinguished
visitors. There were the kings and queens of Italy, Belgium,
Greece, Romania, and Sweden, along with their friend Axel
Munthe. Only Bernard Berenson was missing, but probably he
was not yet quite in the swim, and I had the right man waiting.
He was a civil servant who called once a week to see what I had
found for him. He came up from Whitehall, which he disliked so

much that although I went along to have tea with him for years in the A.B.C. in St. Martin's Lane, I never knew which government office he was in. He collected anything autographed, any manuscript material, and these royalties delighted him. They made a change from the score card of a Test Match in the 1880s, signed by both teams, ten Phil May drawings, a royal pardon of George III, an appeal by John Burns, and a seventeenth-century commonplace book, which, with a collection of literary letters, I suppose should have been reported to the proper collector or library, but I'm still glad that they went to this lonely old boy in his furnished rooms in Clapham.

Some Country Bookshops

The English country booksellers were once an independent lot of men, refusing to be overawed by London, as the French provincial booksellers have always been by Paris. In the 'bad' old days at country sales, they fought, and kept many good books away from London. It is different today with the scarcity of good books, and a wider world market meaning that few local sales escape the big hungry town booksellers. Today then, one can never be sure about finding any books in the country bookshops, but one can be sure that the booksellers themselves are still personalities.

My first country bookshop was J. A. D. Bridger's in Market Jew Street, Penzance, Cornwall. I passed it during a school holiday, did not go in, but for years afterwards, and especially when I became a bookseller myself, I was to remember Mr. Bridger's windows. They were dressed with old pamphlets, and volumes tied open to show early title-pages; through the open door the shop was dark with old calf and morocco. The haunting doubled with the years, and when I came back fifty years later in 1969, the shop was more Cornish but in the style of Sir John Betjeman and Batsford's Shell Guides. The old calf and morocco, even the old boards, had gone for ever.

It was like a bookseller's version of *Un Carnet de Bal*, M. Duvivier's film with its beautiful deflating of nostalgia, but if Cornwall only offered Duvivier, Devon more than made up for it with something more like Fernandel.

Coming back from Cornwall, we had stopped for petrol in Torquay, and the young man at the pumps, seeing a number of old-looking books in the back seat, asked if we had been at the

Eric Blundell's
fifteenth-century
bookshop, Lewes

William Duck's
'The Cupola',
Hastings

'A well known character at Brighton', c.1830, lithograph from a painting by G. M. Brighty

Another well known character at Brighton, George Sexton and his son David, 1972

Moyse brothers? They were round the corner, three cheerful old men, in a small white building, with 'Moyse Brothers Cycle Repairers' painted on the facia. When the gentlemen and ladies of Torquay had bicycled up and down its seven hills, the Moyse brothers had been busy with the spills and strains. Business almost disappeared with the motor-car, and being great readers of books, the brothers decided that they would now deal in them. There were still old bicycles strung up from the roof of the workshop downstairs, but the loft was piled with books. It was tantalizing to see a title one fancied near the foot of one of these stacks, but it would have taken half the afternoon to dismember the stack, and there were the brothers waiting to be entertained. There was not much old calf around; the books had come from little local house sales, and from grateful clients whose machines they had repaired. No rariora, but the Meredith and Eden Phillpotts which a past Torquay had read, were now minor collectors' pieces.

It was two years before I came back. At the petrol station they told me that the eldest brother was dead, and the middle one could only stay at home, and look after things there. Round the corner, there was no-one downstairs; in the November dusk, I was just able to read the notice 'Up the stairs, please'. Upstairs, Fernandel's horse laugh had gone: it was the setting for another French film classic, *Quai des Brumes*. Three hurricane lamps lit the book towers disappearing into the dark, a fourth on a packing case at which a little old man in his duffle coat and beret sat writing. The design for a French film became a Rembrandt etching of the most beautiful bookshop I will ever see. I am sure that I bought a book or two; it was the old man's business and pleasure, but one just wanted to sit beside him and say 'Dear Rembrandt'. Next summer I heard from a dealer in North Devon that the last of the Moyse brothers was dead, and that he had bought their stock.

There was more than one bookseller in North Devon. Edward Carlson was only there for a few years after the last war, and he was the most lively. He had come up with a collection of valuable books which he wanted to deliver himself to a West End bookseller, and staying on for a day or two to poke around the London bookshops, ours was one of the shops he called at. He took away our list of wants and interests, following them up with his miscellaneous offers and very long letters. Before the war he had an import business in Hong Kong, but with that now finished he had come back to this country to be what he had always wanted to be, a secondhand bookseller. His wife and daughter said they would go their own way if he did, and he still became a bookseller. His friend in Westward Ho! was J. H. Taylor who, with Harry Vardon and Sandy Braid, had divided the British and American golf championships between them before the First World War The old man must have been over 90, but still walked with Edward Carlson on his beloved links. When he did visit Westward Ho! with the warning that it was much more bungaloid than Charles Kingsley, it was difficult to find the Carlson address. Far from being one of the bungalows, it was a disused aeroplane hangar out on the Northam marshes. Some sketchy boarding hived off a corner of the hangar where his books, table, bed, oil-lamp and stove were. He was a completely satisfied secondhand bookseller.

Devon and Cornwall have always had the fewest bookshops, so some months ago I was glad to propose, and see, young Bruce Burley with his pleasant shop on the Quay in Truro, become a member of the Antiquarian Booksellers' Association. Sussex, on the other hand, with over fifty secondhand bookshops listed in the Trade Directory, is the most popular county, with Hastings and Brighton as the top towns. Hastings now proclaims a composite advertisement: *A first-class bookshop and three specialist booksellers, bid a cordial welcome to collectors and librarians. All issue catalogues regularly.* The Howes bookshop in Trinity Street with its three floors of books is an old friend; Mr. William Duck, one of the specialists, is a new one who lodges in an Italianate mini-palazzo in Belmont Road. The Cupola was built in 1835 from the designs of Joseph Kay, surveyor to the Foundling and Greenwich Hospitals, and architect to the Post Office. Kay had acquired a taste for the romantic, and the house he was now building for himself was to be based on the Tower of the Winds. The Cupola is the nearest thing to a folly in Sussex which can be actually lived in, and is Hastings's most effective riposte to Brighthelmstone, but it is going to be difficult to dislodge Brighton. One hundred and fifty years of the 'Bon Ton' and trippers from London insisting that everything, including the bookshops, is nicer here beside the sea. There were bookshops in Brighton at the beginning of the last century. In our bookroom here there is a coloured lithograph *circa* 1820, 'A well known Character at Brighton, from a Painting by Mr. G. M. Brighty, miniature Painter to H.R.H. the Princess Auguste.' The Character, a bookseller (still unidentified), stands inside his shop in a pink waistcoat, blue cravat, and long white pinafore, holding a morocco volume in one hand, with a background of shelves of books to which are pinned four large broadsheets. The painting may have been commissioned by the Princess Augusta, because of all the royal family she would have been the only one likely to have poked around the lanes. The sixth child, she never married, and had the gift of making that tension-afflicted family laugh. Mme D'Arblay, giving the princess's family pet name, 'La Coquette corrigée', also tells how she led the singing of *God Save the King* when it was first sung to the King and the Queen in Weymouth, Brighthelmstone's one rival further along the coast.

Today Brighton has another well-known bookseller character, Mr. George Sexton, now easily doyen of the country booksellers, and as such recently honoured with a commemoration dinner by his old fellow booksellers and customers.

When I first met George forty odd years ago, it was in his first shop in North Street, today called Dyke Road. When old Jimmy Thorp gave up his bookshop at 53 Ship Street, originally established in 1868, George moved down there. Now (21 June 1972), George writes that at 83 he feels that it is time to hand over com-. pletely to his son David. It is reassuring to know that future visits to Ship Street will find another old, but younger friend there, but it is good to hear from George that the occasional sunny morning may find him there too. This sense of continuity, and the passing on of old skills being one of the great charms of the antiquarian book trade.

Across the way in Duke Street, George's good neighbour, Mr. Holleyman, is still young enough to be able to live with today's inflationary prices, and old enough to have the tolerance and generosity of the passing generation of antiquarian booksellers.

On my last visit to Brighton, it was to some very different bookshops. I had gone down to spend the day with Graham Greene, and after lunch the bookseller was taken by the author on a tour of his bookshops. These were not in the *Booksellers' Directory*, but in *Brighton Rock* land, i.e. the meaner streets downhill to the left as one comes out of the station. Graham's favourite was 'The Unicorn' which looked most unlikely to a professional. More unlikely still was the owner, a young American in jeans, who had given up Californian sun, the sands, and palms of the Pacific, for the grey English Channel and the shingle, but he said that he loved it all. We were lucky to find him open, because on this first sunny spring day, he was about to shut up shop and take his little ginger cat up to the Downs to enjoy the sun with him. We were given five minutes to look round, which was enough for me, with the shelves and their rows of forgotten early twentieth-century authors, being more Graham's way than mine. I bought the only volume in old calf, very shabby, and with no lettering on the spine, *Poetae minores Graeci, accedunt Observationes Radulphi Wintertoni, Cantabrigiiae, 1684*. Later checking showed that there were copies in the British Museum and in the Cambridge University Library, but not in Bodley, nor in the Henry E. Huntington Library at San Marino, California. A difficult decision between local patriotism and Bodley, or admiration for Californian allegiance to Brighton and the Huntington? In the end both discovered that they did have copies, and it was Graham who benefited from the transaction. Remembering my simple trade trick of making for the shabby old calf volume with no lettering on the spine, he found such a volume on his own shelves. Writing me the details a few weeks later, he cited a scarce Salzburg printed description of the rites in the cathedral there. Mr. Neill, in whom Sir Thomas Bodley can never have had a more devoted servant, would have liked to have added this volume to his Bodleian Library, but Graham is a collector as well as an author.

Between Brighton and Hastings, Eastbourne keeps offering two varieties of bookshop to its 'retired' book collectors. In South Street, there used to be 'Glover and Daughter', with patriarchal Mr. Glover and long white beard in the General Booth manner. When he died, Miss Glover carried on, and the piles of books grew higher and the basement overflowed. There was always the promise of wonderful finds, but it was better, and easier, to sit and talk to Miss Glover. In the parallel Grove Road there was King's bookshop with its elegant chandelier, period bookcases, and a flower arrangement. Eastbourne had its choice. Three years ago, Miss Glover retired, Mr. Raymond Smith came along from Brighton, bought the business, and set to. Today it is all burnish and brightness in South Street, the shelves classified, and labelled, a white-painted basement with 'No smoking please.' Changes all round, but still the old welcome. And then about the same time, Mr. and Mrs. King put up their bookshop in Grove Road for sale. Back here in Oxfordshire, we had a neighbouring farmer who had always bought books, and who was intrigued with a bookseller's life. When the farm was bedded for the night, he would come along to talk books. Looking at our quiet shelves of uncomplaining books, he would sigh as he thought of his herd of eighty, uncomplaining too, but always waiting to be milked. He had asked me to let him know if ever I saw a bookshop which might suit him. I telephoned him when I saw the King advertisement, and he went down to Eastbourne and settled for the shop. When he came across to tell me, I hoped that he was keeping that elegant chandelier, but he replied, 'What chandelier?' Today, Mr. Parmiter stands smiling and happy in the old Glover way among piles of books still to be sorted out and priced. Grove Road and South Street continue to offer a change of air in the same seaside resort.

Between Eastbourne and Hastings, happy in making no claims

at all, and remarkable only for yet another pair of differing book-sellers, is Bexhill. Mr. E. Van Dam is now there in Dorset Road but still only interested in *Black-Letter*, and in *Illuminated Books of Hours*. When I first met him, nearly fifty years ago, it was in the large pillared shop in the Charing Cross Road which later became the Leicester Square Post Office, and is now a pop restaurant with monkeys running up and down the windows. After Charing Cross Road, Mr. Van Dam had a manor-house on the slopes of the Cotswolds above Cheltenham, and now he is as happy as ever in Bexhill in a semi-detached, with an old book sanctum fashioned out of a greenhouse opening off his study. It was splendid seeing how the dedicated bookseller can always adjust. Bexhill's second bookseller is nearer the sea. Last year, parking the car on the front, I saw opposite in Marina Arcade, among the cafés and gift shops, one with a sign 'Shells and Books'. At first it all seemed shells, large pink ones from the Indian Ocean and daintier ones from our Channel, but Miss Gardiner told me that there was a large bookroom downstairs. Theosophy and Mysticism were Miss Gardiner's subjects, but she was sure that somewhere there was an eighteenth-century farming pamphlet I would like. We could not find the pamphlet, and I came away with *The Falls of Clyde, or the Fairies; a Scottish dramatic Pastoral in five Acts, Edinburgh, printed by William Creech, 1806*, which seemed a happy compromise be-tween her mysticism and my farming. But when I got back from the seaside, the farming pamphlet was waiting here, with a triumphant little note from Miss Gardiner.

Seaford, along the coast from Bexhill, is remarkable for the number of its preparatory schools, which during the summer holidays become Summer Schools. In 1922 I went to a Fabian Summer School in one of them, first ate nut cutlets, and Bernard Shaw came down to lecture. Many years later Miss Mary Ranger, after an apprenticeship in the Sanders Bookshop in the High, Oxford, opened her own bookshop in Seaford. It was here that I was always told, 'Never mind the prices, I leave these to you.' Today she has given up the bookshop, but it is always pleasant to call at her pretty little house in the town. Behind Seaford, in the folds of the Downs, is another lady bookseller, Miss O. P. Self, from whom I have never bought a book, which did not matter, as her main interest was in seeing that the little village of Telscombe continued as beautiful as its situation. She had her cottage from the squire on this understanding, and whenever we called she was chasing off visitors picking the daffodils planted along the road through the village.

Behind the Downs, in the county town of Lewes, serious book-selling guaranteed by 'Bow Windows Bookshop', part of the great Dawson bookshop complex. From the outside, this bookshop adds to the distinction of the Georgian broad pavement, plane tree lined Upper High Street. Inside there are always good books, and Mr. and Mrs. Lucas, with Mr. Lucas an old friend of the William Dawson Pilgrim Street days of the twenties and thirties. Lower down the hill, where Georgian ends, is Mr. Eric Blundell in his 'Fifteenth Century Bookshop', one of Lewes's showpieces. More personal nostalgia here, since Eric Blundell had opened his bookshop in Marchmont Street, Russell Square, London, in the same year that I had opened mine in Cecil Court, and he hasn't altered—the same quiet manner, the same carefully pencilled prices in his books (always the sign of the good book-seller), the same ability to please and keep his customers, now the modest gentry of that corner of Sussex. I don't think he regrets the less modest demands of Bloomsbury.

Hawkhurst is just over the county border in Kent, but for Mr. Burman Lowe, it is always, according to Michelin, '*vaut un détour*'. An eye specialist at Bexhill and Hastings, Burman Lowe had come to like his booksellers and their way of life. When he retired some twenty years ago, he decided to become one too. He may now be old, but he is a glowing advertisement for this most sympathetic of trades. He is also the sort of bookseller from whom one is never sure what one will come away with. A sixteenth-century procla-mation? some Bewick wood blocks? an early cookery book? we have brought away all these. Two years ago, and now most remembered, were the two magnificent large framed woodcuts by Christopher de Jeghers after Rubens. Mrs. Diana Parikian, our neighbouring and *sympathique* bookseller friend, seeing them hanging here, kept on pleading. Came the day, when the roof of the little fourteenth-century church here in Emmington needed repairs, and the congregation of a dozen was in difficulties. For a substantial cheque made out to the Rector, Diana could have the woodcuts, and so with the collaboration of three booksellers the roof of St. Nicholas was made watertight. There was an added reason why this should have come about as it did. Manoug and Diana Parikian live in the old rectory at Waterstock, a hamlet five miles from Emmington, but in the eighteenth century both churches were in the living of the Ashursts of Waterstock. Among my own books, I have *The Patriot King displayed in the Life and Reign of Henry VIII, King of England,* by Edward Lewis, M.A., Rector of Waterstock and Emmington, in Oxfordshire, printed for E. and C. Dilly, 1769.

Up to the last war, Hunt's of Norwich was the great name for the eastern counties apart from the university bookshops in Cambridge. By the books that used to flow into Hodgson's from the shop on Orford Hill, Hunt's must have had a wonderful connection in all these counties. I did not get to the shop until during the war, when with my battery stationed in Cromer, I had a Saturday afternoon pass. By then Mr. Hunt was dead, and the shop was run by a very old assistant, 'Hookey Hunt', originally Mr. Hook. It was still the traditional county bookshop, with the twisting staircase up to six or seven small rooms crammed with books, and in each room there was a pair of old boots. I did not like to ask Hookey about this signature tune. He was a most amiable old man who told me that he lived with his mother, but these boots seemed ominous. In these days, Mr. Tom Crowe in St. Giles's splendidly revives the reputation which Hunt's used to give to Norwich for books. From the catalogues he issues, one would guess that it is from the whole country rather than from the county that Mr. Crowe draws his books. Until a few years ago, there was another Norwich book character, Mr. Higgins, who had a small shop in Elm Hill, off Tombland. He was a tall diffident middle-aged man, always with a faint pleased-to-

see-you smile in the corners of his lips. There was a partly cur-
tained glass door at the back of the shop leading into the parlour
where his old father sat in front of the fire and the mother scuttled
around with pots and pans. Tom Crowe once told me how one
of the happiest of his war memories had been on the night when
as duty officer he had been called out to give orders to a new
posting, and there, modestly at the end of the line was Mr. Higgins.
For the time being at least, life became much more pleasant for
Private Higgins.

With Tony Doncaster in his pleasant shop on the North Hill,
Colchester, Essex, one shares a common customer. This happened
after the war when Tony, living round the corner from Cecil
Court, was wondering in which town to open a bookshop. He
came in one day to tell me that he had plumped for Colchester,
and I told him that I had just had a man in from that town who
could be a customer. This man was interested in anthropology,
and as 'interests' I had written 'filthy books' on his card. Doncaster
copied the card and opened his shop. The anthropologist duly
came in, and giving his name, Doncaster felt it was familiar, went
to his file and laid the card between them. The anthropologist
laughed first, Doncaster managed his story, and the anthropologist
was a customer for life.

Between Doncaster and Tom Crowe, there is Mr. Way in
Burrough Green, Suffolk, whom we went to see in case among
his large stock on Huntin', Shootin', and Fishin' there might be
summat on Farmin'. There was, but for once drawing a blank
would not have mattered. Burrough Green had more than books
to offer. Mr. Way lives in the large rectory at the corner of the
green, and the car was led up the drive by a mixed pack of spaniels
and terriers. It was reassuring to find four cats sitting at the front
door paying no attention to all the yapping and tail-waving.
Mr. Way also paid no attention. A tall bearded man in knicker-
bockers, he might be out of Trollope's *Hunting Sketches*—or
maybe with the Cambridge M.A. and the slight stoop, some
nineteenth-century sporting don? After the books, we were taken
the rounds. First the famous county pack of Bassett hounds, then

the Welsh ponies in the paddock. On the way someone called 'Hen' was spoken to, and then carried around perched on Mr. Way's shoulder. But if he had 'Hen', I had a black cat whom I had also spoken to, and insisted on the tour balancing from one shoulder to the other. If only one could have taken the visit as perfectly normal in the way that Mr. Way did so placidly.

Lincolnshire, the emptiest of the English shires, was emptiest of books too. The shop in the cobbled lane leading up to Lincoln cathedral always promised, but I never found a book there. A bookshop in Louth flickered for a few years, but as I discovered thirty-odd years ago, this was the most provoking and fascinating of the shires. It was while making a sweep down across the Wolds that we came to see Boston and the Stump, and found the bookshop beside the canal. With the gasworks across the canal, it was T. S. Eliot *Wasteland*, but a couple of rows of old calf in the window made it look like bookseller's land too. Again it was Lincolnshire, and the calf ended in a doubtful handful more to cheer up the owner whose grandson had been drowned the week before in the canal opposite. A few weeks later Graham Greene came into Cecil Court to tell me about a walking tour with his brother Hugh through Lincolnshire. They too had come to Boston and been directed to the bookshop by the canal, and they too had felt we must be the only ones to come here. In the end, Graham found a pleasant early eighteenth-century two-volume edition of Nathaniel Lee to add to his collection of seventeenth-century dramatists, at that time one of his main interests. If they wondered why there was not more, the owner was to explain when he said, 'Funny, I had another gent from London here last week, Mr. David Low.' But the other gent had slipped up on Nathaniel Lee.

Emmington is strategically placed for some of the pleasantest book runs in the country, and the favourite is over the Cotswolds to visit Alan Hancox in Cheltenham. His shop at the end of the tree-shaded Parade, the nearest we come in England to the Cours Mirabeau in Aix-en-Provence, has a Provençal air too. Alan Hancox is unique among booksellers in having a pair of hands that never seem to stop adding new settings for his sympathetically selected books. The morning in the good but fading manners of Cheltenham, then across the Severn valley to spend the afternoon with John and Sylvia Walter and their books at Much Markle, under the western slopes of the Malvern hills. Their home 'Hellens' is a red-brick Tudor manor, with part of the earlier house, including the small banqueting hall, still there. It was in this banqueting hall, on the night of 20 September 1327, that Queen Isabella and Mortimer plotted the murder of Edward II the following day at Berkeley. There are no ghosts this afternoon as John Walter shows the Elizabethan knot garden he is uncovering, and Sylvia asks about the Bourbon roses she plans in the new rose garden, and we promise to bring along a 'Zéphirine Drouhin' in the autumn. We do get down to looking at books in the end, but that has interruptions when someone notices that the flock of Chinese geese have struggled up from the meadow and are rampaging about the garden.

The second favourite book run is up the Thames valley through Kelmscott to Cirencester and the Burtons' bookshop. The Old House, Gloucester Street, now offers books instead of the wool which one of the town merchants was selling in the seventeenth century. Earlier, in pre-Reformation days, the Old House had also been in the wool trade, as one of the mills belonging to the Augustinian monks with an abbey in the town. The little stream running through the garden was their mill stream, but it had been cut much earlier by the Romans to supply the south part of their Corinium with water. The morning with the Burtons in this old Roman capital and medieval wool town, then south through Malmesbury to the gentler Wiltshire and Richard Hatchwell's books, because 'bookshop' somehow doesn't fit Richard Hatchwell. His address is the Old Rectory, Little Somerford, with its atmosphere of some lost Victorian Sunday. Maybe it is related to the lunch with the well-behaved children whom one has seen as babies, and to whom now, as great uncle bookseller, one brings boiled sweets? The books too are a gentle collection of minor eighteenth- and early nineteenth-century masters, with Wiltshire a special branch, and in its celebration a fascinating catalogue on

Stonehenge, with the books arranged in the chronological order of the theories and conclusions that they represent. Wiltshire is proud to be housing the most important prehistory monument in western Europe.

Nearer humility and the spirit of the Old Rectory is Richard's last catalogue: *Mary Russell Mitford (1787–1855), Her Books and Her Friends*. Few booksellers would hazard a catalogue on such a minor literary writer as Mary Russell Mitford. In his preface, Richard gives his reason: 'She brought to life with wit, humour, and animation, what must have been a rather dull and beggarly world.' That was the reason, too, for the many devoted friendships among her contemporaries, including Coleridge, Lamb, Charles Kingsley, Mrs. Trollope, and Mrs. Browning. Near her death, Walter Savage Landor's verses in praise of her 'plasant tales' ended: 'Nor even there could any tell the country's purer charm so well as Mary Mitford.' This Miss Mitford gathering is a welcome change from the too many catalogues of these days studded with rather meaningless high-spots at very meaningful prices, and never for one item coming to life.

As excuse for seeing the New Forest in each of the four seasons, there is an old friend Mr. H. J. Mack right in its heart, and later friends, David and Doreen Pratt at Dibdin Purlieu on Southampton Water. For neighbours at King's Ground, Mr. Mack has the red deer, beautiful to see in the moonlight, but not the kindest of visitors for his garden. For his booksellers visitors, Mr. Mack continues to do his best, but it becomes harder every year. On our last visit came the sad 'I'm afraid I have nothing you would really like'. Then over coffee, the confession, 'This week I did buy a book, but I like it so much'. The book was fetched: Randle Holme's *Storehouse of Armory . . . with the Instruments used in all Trades and Sciences, 1701*. But as the *Cambridge Bibliography of English Literature* points out: 'Armory is quite misleading, as this is in fact a diffused collection of miscellaneous information about a well-equipped man's general needs and gear in an active life.' Even this amplification of the title does not do justice to the large folio which is a fascinating contemporary picture of the practical life of the men and women of the seventeenth century, with each of the many plates showing on average seventy of the tools used by cooks, husbandmen, masons, pewterers, printers, weavers, etc., etc.

At the end in his 'To the Reader', Randle Holme, 'Sewer of the Chamber to Charles II', writes, 'The book is ready for the press, and wants nothing but encouragement for the times are so hard, trading so dead, money scarce, paper wanting, wages great.' Fifty years later, Dr. Johnson read this Address, and 'it suggested to him the idea of his own inimitable preface to his dictionary' (W. T. Lowndes).

Mr. Mack's coffee became cold as one dipped and looked. It was forgotten when Mr. Mack most generously said, 'Since you find the book so fascinating, it's yours'.

David and Doreen Pratt have different surprises at The Bookery. A few years ago it was helping to dig out the car somehow bedded in the rose border. On a later visit the chimney caught fire and any idea of looking at books also went up in smoke. But Doreen remains faithful with the periodic book lists, full of original titles and spelling. In a recent letter there was her charming assessment, 'We are muddlers I admit, but who wants a greatly efficient Antiquirian Bookseller?' A few years ago, sponsoring the Pratt application for membership of that very efficient but human Association of Antiquarian Booksellers, their election did seem a triumph for both parties.

Richard Booth in Hay-on-Wye, Brecon, Wales, is a whole day expedition. As it involves an early morning start, it is for summer days only, but it also means that once over the river Severn, and through the Forest of Dean, it isn't England any longer. Except for the ironmongers on most of the corners, Hay-on-Wye might be any little market town on the Dordogne. The Booth castle, high on its mound in the centre of the town, and invisible from below behind its screen of trees, is another agreeable surprise. The castle itself eminently habitable, with a dozen or so rooms in the centre, and the ruins of the original Norman building on either flank. From the lawn on the front, one looks up into the Black Mountains, and from the walls behind, across the Wye to the Welsh hills. On my last visit there were lots and lots of books, but the deal which I think made us both happiest was the exchange of all our books on Wales for a seventeenth-century carved armoire. With so much history around him Richard Booth would never miss this piece, and we have never missed the books on Wales. We had gone to Stratford on Avon for *Henry IV, Part Two*, and discovered Mr. Jaggard's bookshop in Sheep Street. His name, the name of the street, the little shop in the sixteenth-century building, are all so completely right, and Mr. Jaggard had done nothing to spoil, or to cash in. An old cast of the Shakespeare bust in the chancel of the parish church stood in the centre of the window, but that was his one concession to 'belonging'. The shop was full, and Mr. Jaggard was busy taking the shillings off the different nationals and age groups. One almost sensed the notice 'Please no collectors or booksellers', but he was politely understanding, and we were waved to the gallery at the end of the shop. There were stacks of dusty pamphlets, but no-one else, not even any of the ladies from the Folger Library. Coming down with our pamphlets we had to wait while a young German girl tried to explain to Mr. Jaggard that she wanted this book, but could not afford it. He looked at it, and must have made some reduction, because she went off with it smiling. One came out of Mr. Jaggard's shop feeling that this was probably the single feature in the town which would have pleased William Shakespeare, and one was glad that it was a bookshop.

Today, Oxford is almost on one's doorstep; fifty years ago, cycling out to lunch in Chinnor took an hour. Today, remembering the undergraduate's account I opened with Blackwell's in 1922, they must be my Number One Oxford bookseller, however splendid the transformation of the years in between. The great Norrington Room, and all the light and air at 50/51 Broad Street, where I recall the small odd rooms and the dusty corners. The million-pound project steadily rising in the west of the city. Blackwell's Exports, Blackwell's Publishers, and all the associated bookshops: almost certainly the greatest bookselling complex in this, or indeed in any other country.

I am glad that the antiquarian book department with my old

friend Edward East in charge, has been moved to Oxford's old traditional Ship Street, where yards of old calf and morocco do not have to look sadly at miles of dust wrappers. The ease and semi-obscurity at Ship Street are specially welcome in one's old university city where there are so many ghosts. Ghosts however who become seven young champions as Edward talks of the famous all-international back division in the Varsity rugby team of 1923, a team we both saw playing at the Iffley Road ground. No ghosts either, when Edward caps my Blackwell 1922 account with that of his older friend, Sir Keith Feiling, Kt. My old Christ Church Student, and Chichele Professor of Modern History started his Blackwell account in 1902, and today it is still as active as is Sir Keith Feiling himself.

Today the sense of the past is left to J. Thornton and Son, University Booksellers, at 11 Broad Street, and how naturally they sustain it. The shop window not laid out—just full of books. The narrow old shop shelved from floor to ceiling, with two twisting staircases up the three floors with the sixteen rooms above unchaperoned most of the time, a real act of faith in these days. The staff in the traditional bookshop's years of service. Mr. Wild, the manager, always being asked for in affection and trust by visiting librarians, collectors, and booksellers. Elderly gentlemen scribbling endless memos in odd corners. At the back of the shop, in the raised counting house window, two ladies perched side by side. It would have been no surprise to see them wearing the elbow to wrist glacé leather protectors of the Dickensian counting house clerk, or to see one of them reaching up to send a receipt travelling down the shop on an overhead pneumatic wire. Alongside the counting house, Mr. Jack Thornton slides on and off his high stool, keeping the wheels oiled, just as he must do with his bicycle, because he would never dream of running the motor-car which keeps on destroying his Oxford. He is 'Mr. Jack' to the older ones in the firm, 'Young Mr. Thornton' to the older customers and friends, for Mr. Thornton (senior) died five years ago, aged over 90, and in the shop to the end. From 'Young Mr. Thornton', the story told him by his grandfather, of how he used to sit with his father (great-grandfather Thornton) in the door of their shop in the High watching the drovers bringing the cattle and sheep up that cobbled street on their way to the market. The Thornton bookshop had been started by this great-grandfather in 1835 in the High, between All Souls and the Queen's College. No wonder that Mr. John Sparrow, Warden of All Souls, made Mr. Jack promise never to alter anything at J. Thornton and Son, University Booksellers.

Cambridge with its good university bookshops, but with the departure of Gustave David has none today with the mystique of Oxford's J. Thornton and Son. Instead Cambridge offers unique bookshop history, because at 1 Trinity Street, the home of Bowes and Bowes, there has always been a bookshop since 1581. The firm have very kindly given me the story of this, the longest-lived bookshop in Great Britain.

William Scarlett, the bookseller who was charged before the Court of the Star Chamber with pirating the Countess of Pembroke's *Arcadia*, was there at Trinity Street, Cambridge, from 1581 until 1617, and from then until 1843 there were eleven different owners. In 1843 came two young Scotsmen, Daniel and Alexander Macmillan, and in addition to bookselling they began to lay the foundations of what was to become one of the largest publishing houses in the world.

Daniel Macmillan, the grandfather of Mr. Harold Macmillan, was so knowledgeable about books and such a Carlylean personality that many of the University dons became not only customers but friends, and the bookshop became something of an unofficial University literary club. Tennyson gave a reading of 'Maud' in what was then the drawing-room on the first floor. Thackeray lunched with the Macmillans when he was lecturing on the English humorists. Charles Kingsley was a frequent visitor, and in an extant letter-book is a communication dated 12 June 1862, giving instructions to the printers about setting-up *The Water Babies*.

Daniel Macmillan died in 1857, and a year later the growth of the publishing side made a London office necessary. This was at first managed by Robert Bowes, a nephew of the Macmillans, but soon Alexander Macmillan moved to London to devote the whole of his time to publishing, while young Robert Bowes came back to Cambridge to run the bookshop now known as Macmillan and Bowes. Like his uncles and Thomas Carlyle, Robert Bowes was blessed, or cursed, with that peculiarly Scottish zest for educating himself. He may have been living in Cambridge, but that is what he did, becoming in addition such a bibliographical authority, that the University showed their respect and admiration by making him an Honorary M.A. His son, George Brimley Bowes, became a partner in 1899 when the firm finally became the present Bowes and Bowes.

When I first visited the bookshop in the early thirties one heard about a Major Bowes, but to a young bookseller he seemed the kind of legendary figure who must not be disturbed. But in the forty years since then, there have been fewer qualms about disturbing the shop serenity at 1 Trinity Street.

Trinity Street also has Deighton, Bell & Co., still at No. 13, but today without that other semi-legendary figure and friend Percy Babington, and now part of the William Dawson complex. Heffer's are now also in Trinity Street after their recent move from the old-time shop in Petty Cury to the splendid new premises at 20 Trinity Street.

Beside these three big names, there are three others to be remembered, maybe in a minor but certainly in a personal and affectionate key. First, Mr. and Mrs. Pearson, in their book parlour at the end of Hobson Street, a unique combination of town and gown, with Mr. Pearson (M.A., Cantab.), the son (a rowing blue), and their callers, academic, lay, or trade, still certain that of all antiquarian booksellers Mrs. Pearson was the most charming. Then there was the incomparable David, slouching beside his stall in the Market Place, and old Mr. Porter in the top room at Galloway and Porter's in Sidney Street, a six-blossom sweet pea in his button-hole throughout the summer. It *had* to be six blossoms, as young Mr. Porter recently told me. Like Mr. and Mrs. Pearson, these last two characters are now only memories, but it

is good to find young Mr. Porter still in Sidney Street, and young
David either in the Market Place, or in his nearby shops.

A pity that no Etonian has left a picture of Mrs. Brown and her
bookshop at 87 High Street, Eton. The old lady would not have
felt at home in Harold Acton's *Memoirs of an Aesthete*, but Cyril
Connolly must have started his collecting there, and what a picture he might have drawn!

Mr. and Mrs. Brown started their book business in Bayswater
in 1893, moving it down to Eton in the early twenties. Mr. Brown
died shortly after the move and Mrs. Brown carried on with the
business under a new tradition, 'Old Ma Brown's'. She had to give
up in 1953, selling the business to Mr. Bernard Simpson, but the
'Old Ma Brown' embonpoint doesn't fade easily, like some old
soldier's. Today Mr. Simpson still receives letters from old
Etonians addressed 'Old Ma Brown, at 87 High Street, Eton'.
From the College, too, there are memos to the same legend.

My own memory is just as enduring, the stately figure in
crinkly black satin, the silver chain swinging down on the big
bosom, the white high-piled-up hair, the laugh somewhere between Marie Lloyd's and Mae West's. Coloured plate flower
books were her passion. The windows of the shop were filled with
them, laid open at some brilliant plate, and tied with pink tape.
She knew nothing of the bibliography that during the last twenty
years has been given to these books by experts like Mr. Handasyde
Buchanan. By present-day prices, hers were abysmal, but she
couldn't resist these books. One guessed that she was *très* snob, but
one was always received very graciously, and business always ended
with a conducted tour through the little garden behind the shop
to her final surprise, her miniature wishing well. With a fellow
bookseller, she probably felt that she could relax, and be her real
'Old Ma Brown' self. For visits of the sons of the especially rich or
famous, it was 'Good morning young Sir, and will you partake of
a glass of sherry?' Visits from the parents must have meant that she
had the most socially distinguished visiting list in the bookselling
world. Bernard, and Mrs. Simpson, have done what they could
to embalm the old lady, but now with No. 88 added to 87, the

handsome bookcases, one of the best stocks of rare books outside London, and the prices, the old lady would have had palpitations. She would not have approved of today's permissiveness, i.e. one afternoon I heard a gentle wrangle between Mrs. Simpson and an angelic Etonian urchin wanting to swop a pair of grubby gym shoes for a book he could not afford; but she would have approved of Mrs. Simpson's understanding firmness, and of the rows of lovingly signed photographs from her Etonian admirers. Looking at these decorative urchins, and their seniors striding, oblivious, down the High Street, one was not surprised to hear from a group of French girls, the awed *Regardez*! The late M. de Gaulle might be insisting *Non*, but the heart of France seeing these beautiful gilded insolents was shouting *Entrez*!

Some Country Bookshops
Scottish

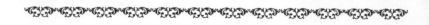

While Edinburgh has always had the tradition for the best book-shops, Glasgow claimed the best bookseller in Hugh Hopkins. This 'Quaritch of the North' was dead when I came back to Scotland, but his son Billy was still in the old shop in Exchange Square. After the last war, Billy moved the business to his home in one of the old city crescents. It was almost home to me too, as I had been born in the adjoining crescent with the added sense of belonging that Flora, his wife, and I had both been christened in the same year in the same Westbourne kirk. It was sometimes difficult to forget Will Fyffe's 'dear auld toun', and keep to books.

If Hugh Hopkins was once Scotland's number one bookseller, James Glen was Glasgow's own. A shoemaker with a life interest in the history of the working-class movement in Scotland; from collecting books and pamphlets on the movement, he finally became a bookseller. He was an old man when I met him, and delighted to hear that I was publishing catalogues on social and economic history in the nineteenth century. James Glen may not have appreciated a Ricardo rarity, but Robert Owen and the Glasgow cotton spinners were part of his life. The London book-seller may have been able to give the Ricardo rarity its proper price, but James Glen's approach I will always remember as beyond price. His widow still carries on, with the books still far too cheap, but it would have been useless to say, 'What about inflation?'; she and her manager, Mr. Macleod, would just have laughed with an 'Och Aye! but we're nae worrit'. I did try to

Ian Grant,
chief of the clan
of Scottish
antiquarian
booksellers

Madame
Christian de Sèze,
*première
bouquiniste
du Périgord*

Count Potocki of
Montalk, drypoint
by Komjati, 1935

His
bookseller,
1950

make up a little, by saying that down home I had quite a few Scottish books, and what about sending these up to them? A tea chest was packed and sent, with a note suggesting that they credit me with what these books are worth to them against my next visit. A week later an appreciative reply and a cheque because it was against all their principles to owe money. While the cheque just about covered the cost of the carriage, they were completely right in their arithmetic. I just had to make a mental note not to buy back any of my Scottish books on my next visit.

In its bookshops as in everything, Edinburgh was as beautiful and serious as Glasgow was lovable, and before the war what a grand show these Edinburgh bookshops made! John Grant on George IV Bridge, with the showrooms downstairs and above, five large rooms opening out one from another in an endless display of packed shelves. James Thin on 'The Bridges' with more mysterious little rooms and corners in the basement and upstairs; the bookshop for ministers of the Church of Scotland and the university professors. Brown in swankier George Street, with a background of tartan and the county collectors. Alexander Brunton, in his semi-basement in Hanover Street, more remote, but most knowledgeable of them all. Douglas and Foulis, then with an Antiquarian Department in Castle Street, and the 'Scots Grey' troopers, William Dunlop, the Baxendines, Bob Aitken, Cairns, and Hogg. But what first struck and pleased, was the Edinburgh 'caller' air that blew through its trade, as well as round its bookshops.

After London's closer, secretive atmosphere, one appreciated the generous touches from one bookseller after another, who would say, 'Have you been to Mr. So and So? Weel, you must, and I'll just give him a ring to be sure he is there.' Refreshing too seeing them coming out from an auction at Dowell's Sale Rooms where they had been fiercely bidding against each other, and now going off for a friendly dram. The generosity too of these bosses to so many of their assistants who went on to open their own bookshops, with the bosses continuing to help and advise, and strangest of all to Sassenach eyes, an assistant in the morning, who opened his own shop after lunch. The 10 per cent discount may have been worked out to a penny on one's bills, but these Edinburgh booksellers were only in the tradition of the Scot who may be careful about his pence but is always generous in the things that matter.

Outside these two cities, there was a little more to the Scottish bookshops, but not very much, with the pleasures and surprises being more in the scenery getting to them. In a small shop in Dunoon, the proprietor said, 'What a peety ye were no here last week.' From his description of the large old calf folio with its 'grand' maps, it sounded like John Speed's *Prospect of the World*, and one did not have the heart to ask the old man what he had got for it. In the bookshop in Newtonmore one was in time for a presentation copy of the first edition in the original boards of *The Poems of Mrs. Grant of Laggan*. Unfortunately it was bought by a visitor here, before there was time for a catalogue note. Laggan is a village a few miles west of Newtonmore, and Mrs. Grant was the widow of the minister there. Left with a young family of eight, she decided to bring them up by writing, learned the Gaelic, and recorded in letters and notes the life she saw being lived by the crofters on Speyside. Published in three volumes in 1806, these *Letters from the Mountains* were such a success that Mrs. Grant moved down to Edinburgh, where the children were properly educated, and she queened it among the literati for the rest of her life. These *Poems* of 1803 were her first publication, and because she had them printed for herself, cautiously, and in a small edition, they are very scarce. With a family tradition for summer holidays at Mains' Hotel, Newtonmore, going back to my grandparents' days in the eighteen-nineties, there were still many of the old people left, but no-one could identify the man or the family to whom Mrs. Grant had inscribed this copy.

Perth was a problem in the Sir James Barrie manner. Two brothers Deuchar had shops opposite each other in South Street. They had not spoken for years, so one could not visit both! The one on the east side of the street was kind, but did not have many books. The one on the west side had not only a shop full of books, but a cavern stacked with books up the neighbouring wynd. Unfortunately a cheque was 'nae guid to him', nor was any packing up, much less dispatch by post, or rail. Aberdeen did have the James Bissett bookshop, then opposite the Marischal College, but more tempting was 'Low's Book Stall' in the galleries of the Fish Market, with books straggling down the whole length of the old iron gallery. I was too shy to ask if we might not have a common ancestor, and when I went back after the war old Low was dead, his daughter had rented a shop in Union Street, and got rid of the shabby old books in the market. The shop was bright and tidy, and very, very dull. Alastair Steven's was a pleasant meeting with Scottish Nationalism in its more acceptable enthusiasms. We had been corresponding about the Scottish magazine *Speirin* which he edits, and then spent an evening with him among his books in Blairgowrie, Angus. Next morning we took him along with us on our way north over the Grampians to Speyside, dropping him at Dunkeld, where he strode off with the large rucksack of books on his shoulders. Scotland still has one kilted colporteur.

For the future of antiquarian and secondhand bookselling in Scotland, it is comforting to have stories of two other booksellers. They are Cyril Barrow and Sydney Stansfield, who both decided that England was too crowded for proper living. Scotland might be a risk in the making of a living by selling books, but they both took the chance. Today they write to me, Cyril Barrow from the Border country (Leitholm, by Coldstream, Berwickshire), and Stansfield from way up north (Fortrose, the Black Isle, Ross-shire), both saying the same things, 'Braw air and books, and guid folk'.

But to end with two 'guid scottie' friends, Kulgin Duval and Colin Hamilton, who in recent years have been adding much purple to Scottish antiquarian bookselling with a series of scholarly catalogues, mainly on the Scottish eighteenth-century scene. Their last, *Scott and his Scotland*, beautifully printed by Stamperia Valdonega, Verona, having the added attraction that the books are to be seen at their new home, Frenich, a historic Perthshire farm-house on the shores of lovely Loch Tummel.

Some Country Bookshops
Irish

Hodges Figgis and Co., and Greene's Library are the Dublin bookshops I remember in the thirties, and both are still there, although
both at new addresses, and Greene's Library has become Greene &
Co., with Bertie Pembrey, the present owner, having the most
harmonious personality of any bookseller I know. But such steady
going on was not what one expected from Irish booksellers after
an earlier meeting with the late Townley Searle. Townley had
opened his first bookshop on Lower Ormond Quay just after
the First World War, and issued his catalogue No. 1 in 1919,
with this prefatory note: 'A speciality is made of items relating to
particular trades and callings.' Townley seems to have anticipated
by forty years the present English book trade's passion for Industrial Archaeology. He was probably too much of a pioneer for
Dublin, because two years later he was in London where his
pioneering was to give much joy until the Second World War put
a stop to his kind of jollification. Townley's first pitch in London
was the Montmartre Gallery, a narrow cavern of a shop next
door to Willie Clarkson's in Wardour Street, Shaftesbury Avenue.
Willie Clarkson, as the greatest of all English theatrical costumiers
and wig-makers, had a star-studded clientele which did not amuse
Townley. They drifted into his Gallery to pick up this and that,
and lay it down when they were told the price, although they
did add 'How amusing!' And if they did decide to buy, Townley could never be sure of his money, so he passed over the
Montmartre Gallery to a friend, and moved round the corner to a

top flat in Gerrard Street. Here in an arrangement, part book-shop, part domestic dwelling, and part Buddhist temple, he was able to get down to his other interests, a bibliography of the printed scores of the Gilbert and Sullivan operas, and to Chinese cookery books. Now too, he had time for his troop of Chinese Boy Scouts, to whom he was devoted. As ' 'onolable scout master', he wore an Irish kilt. If only he had looked like one of the tough Irish now building the motorways, but he was a small man with knobbly knees.

Old Massey, another Dublin bookseller with his shop on the Quays, had another kind of Irish charm. When Peter Murray Hill and I went to his shop in 1939 he sat watching while we ran over the shelves, then asked, 'You booksellers from England?' Five minutes later he said that he was tired and going home, brought out a key, and smiled for the first time at our rather surprised 'Goodbye'. Admiring the view along the Liffey a hundred yards up, we saw old Massey cross back across the Quay and open up his shop.

Another Dublin bookseller more than made up for old Massey's welcome. A few years ago, he phoned up one morning to say that there was a sale in Dublin with all my favourite kind of books, the view was next day, so I must come across at once. A place on the afternoon flight was booked on Aer Lingus, and he was waiting, with a hotel booked. Unfortunately, it was St. Patrick's Day, and with all bars closed the hotel dining room was filled with relays playing with biscuits and drinking stout, but we did finally get a picnic in the writing room. At the view next morning there were some interesting books, but if they were in more than one volume, these volumes could be spread through any number of lots. To wait for the sale would have meant chasing these volumes from maybe unco-operative buyers. I left my friend to do his best at the sale, and went along to the airport for the evening flight home. At the airport wisps of fog and an announcement that passengers would be taken by train to Belfast, and on to Heathrow. At least my old friend André Simon was among the passengers; he was then, nearly 90; he had published his first book *The History of the*

Champagne Trade in England in 1905, and talked books all the way up to Belfast, and then slept through the flight.

A dash of inherited Irish magic lifts the load on any otherwise steady English bookseller. I first met Mr. Edward Finneron in the mid thirties in his bookshop at the foot of North Street, Guildford.

At that time, he was dividing his time between the bookshop and his duties with the Brigade of Guards at Pirbright. Three lively sons playing games with the books and the customers enlivened the bookshop when dad was on duty. When the war came, the three boys at once joined up, and when it was over they stuck to dad's army and all three have had brilliant careers in it.

After the war, dad now on his own took the bookshop for a few years to Woking, and then returned to his old home at Brookwood, a few miles from Pirbright. There he happily continues with the occasional book-list but happier still to welcome old customers and friends.

Now at 77 he is still almost as active as I remember him nearly forty years ago in the old North Street shop. If there is a miracle here, one guesses that Mrs. Finneron has a very large part in it. Mr. Finneron may see to the buying, but together they play equal parts in the less spectacular packing and invoicing of the books. The only minor discord I have ever noticed was on our last visit when Mr. Finneron declared, 'What would make me really happy would be buying another large library', and Mrs. Finneron joined in, 'But Edward, what about all these books we have lying around the house?' Women are too sensible to make good booksellers.

Some Country Bookshops
French

The International Directory of Antiquarian Booksellers lists 80 book-shops in London, and 146 throughout the rest of Great Britain, but in the French section, Paris is shown with 130 bookshops and the provinces with 87. Among the 43 display advertisements in the English section, 32 are for London bookshops and 11 for country bookshops, while of the 36 French advertisements, 35 are for Paris bookshops, with M. Henri Rossignol of Les Arcs-sur-Argens, Var. alone representing the provincial booksellers. For the antiquarian book trade, France virtually means Paris *seul*, and knowing all of the 67 Départements south of the Loire one can confirm this ungenerous Parisian boast. Returning to France each year for the past eighteen years, it has always been anywhere south of the Loire, with an occasional détour into Brittany, and an invariable détour around Paris. 'Time off' in France was too precious to be spent with 130 'too with it' booksellers in Paris, and the 87 bookshops in the provinces at least made splendid posting stages all over that beautiful country. They may not have had many rare books, but their owners became old friends, and they knew the best modest hotels, still one of France's minor glories. From corner to corner, the bookshops from Quimper (Finistère) to Nice (Alpes Mar.), and from Dijon (Côte d'Or) to St. Jean de Luz (Bas. Pyrénées), and in between, those in the Charente, Auvergne, Languedoc, Prov-ence, and the valleys of the Loire, Dordogne, Lot, and Tarn. To expect beautiful books too would be asking too much, and indeed I can only remember these in Lyon, in the two bookshops in

Nantes, in the house of Raoul Vergne in Nîmes and best of all in
that of M. Pierre Brun in Pélisanne (Bouches du Rhône). But even
if one was not asking for beautiful books, it seemed strange that in
a large town like Bordeaux the stocks of antiquarian books were so
far below what one would have expected to see in Bristol, the
English equivalent. Bordeaux may have been a disappointment
with its books, but one will always be grateful to the bookseller
there, who recommended the Auberge Basque in Castillon-la-
Bataille 45 kilometres up the Dordogne. M. Jean Aycoberry, the
patron, did the cooking; during the war he had been chef to
General de Gaulle, but the only English he had learned during his
years in London was 'Good morning, 'ow are you? I loave you',
and this was his greeting throughout the day. Madame did the
waiting, 'Belle Mère' the accounts and the bar, and the *jeune fille*
did the rest. There were seven bedrooms, a large dining room
overflowing on Sundays, also a smaller dining room for private
entertaining, because M. Jean's cooking brought parties even from
Bordeaux. As usual there was no bathroom, but with hot and cold,
and a bidet in each of the bedrooms, most English visitors would
be quite happy, though some maybe not so happy with the
lavatory (flush), across the court. But it was all *très, très propre,*
and the charge (autumn, 1971), was 25 francs full pension, three-
course lunch and dinner, and a passable *vin ordinaire.*

M. Jean knew everyone in the little town, and most of the
valley down to Bordeaux and up to Bergerac. When he realized
that we liked to see books, he arranged afternoon outings to some
of his *'antiquaire'* friends. From one of these in St. Emilion there
was a splendid book *Les Aventures extraordinaires d'un Savant russe,*
Paris, 1889. Two volumes, large octavo, many illustrations, with
some showing the equipment with which the Russian savant did
his moon walk in the eighties. The sub-title to the first volume was
La Lune, and to the second *Le Soleil et les petites planètes.* The first
temptation was to offer the romance to Cape Kennedy, allowing
for a library and a sense of humour there, but there was our old
collector friend Professor Robert Lee Wolff in Cambridge, Mass.,
to whom it would be a joy, if he did not already have a copy in

his great collection of nineteenth-century fiction. He did not, and
was delighted, and so was M. Jean, though a little puzzled about
such excitement over such an ordinary-looking book. He took us
up to see the Château de Montaigne because his friend M. le
Boucher had his vineyard on the slopes below the chateau. We
were to visit the chateau, and then join M. et Mme Aycoberry,
M. et Mme Boucher, M. et Mme Pâtisserie at what they said
was a picnic and what we found was an afternoon of M. le
Boucher's wines. M. Jean was also proud to take us to a chateau
near Bergerac where there was a *bibliothèque quelque chose d'extra-
ordinaire* whose owner was one of M. Jean's private diners. The
library was the normal French collector's yard after yard of
maroquin doré, but it is always shaming and uplifting to be received
with French elegance. Later we were able to post out to Bergerac
some handsome-looking volumes about nothing very much.

There was one private library in the town which M. Jean said
we must see. It belonged to an admiral, a great friend of his, but
the evening before the visit the local gendarme came up in the
hotel bar to advise against this. The admiral's flagship had been
sunk by *les Anglais* at Dakar during the last war, and he was sure
that M. l'Amiral had not forgotten.

Among the booksellers, M. Elie Pailloux of La Rochelle was the
most formidable, the most traditional, and even if there were no
'Hamilcar' he could have stepped out of Anatole France. He did
not have a bookshop, and we were indebted to one of the two
lady booksellers in Angers for the introduction. Les Dames
d'Angers were an affectionate joke among their brother booksellers. The younger was almost a scholar bookseller but the elder
liked her wine and disliked her English customers. On the first
visit it was *défendu* even to touch a book, and then she said that she
was leaving *tout de suite* for La Baule. Two years later, we were
allowed to touch a book, and then she announced that she had to
leave for *la Toilette*, but before locking the shop door she
weakened and suggested that we visit her old friend M. Pailloux
in La Rochelle.

M. Pailloux lived in one of the eighteenth-century houses,

which with the arcades, and the hotels built by the wealthy merchants in the early French-Canadian trade, to me make La Rochelle
the most attractive town in France. Two large reception rooms on
the ground floor were his *bibliothèque* and *atelier*. The *bibliothèque* was shelved from floor to ceiling with sixty-odd years'
buying at local sales. In the *atelier* there were cases of coins, rows
of metal dies and stamps, and portfolios of maps and prints. He
was over 80 when we first met him, always in a dark serge suit,
high stiff collar, and white tie. After the business of books, we went
into the dark, mahogany cupboarded kitchen where his sister-in-
law, who kept house for him, sat crocheting. She never said a
word during any of these visits, but after pouring out a glass of his
special *pineau*, M. Pailloux did. He was not the recluse one had
first imagined; he had a chateau and vineyards in the Charente,
but preferred to live in his old town house. The last time we saw
him, we were shown the album of the family groups at a grand-
daughter's wedding to an Italian count. It had been a very grand
affair at the cathedral, and the Pope had sent a nuncio all the way
from Rome in a Rolls-Royce.

While M. Pailloux could never resist an old book, his real pride
was in the one he had written and published himself, *Orfèvres et
Poinçons XVIIe–XIXe Siècles; Poitou, Angoumois Aumis, Saintonge,
Librairie Pailloux, La Rochelle*, 1962. The work was in a limited
edition of 420 copies, quarto, printed on a locally woven hand-
made paper, with 15 plates and numerous reproductions of the
old goldsmiths' marks, and the price was 435 francs (NF). He
knew that this was not our kind of book, but as we were leaving,
he came out with a copy which he handed through the car window
as a *cadeau*. To give an adequate thank you, I had a leaflet printed
and sold fifteen copies to libraries and museums in this country
and in America. The old man was delighted. Last summer when
we called, it was to hear that M. Pailloux had died six weeks
earlier. His daughter, whom we met for the first time, told
us that her father had taken with him into the hospital the
manuscript of the more massive sequel, a history of all the French
goldsmiths and their marks, but had died before he could finish

it. She was now arranging that this should be done. He would
not have agreed with one's description of him as one of the last
representatives of the old traditional France. One can almost hear
the protest 'Mais non, un véritable Charentais'.

From our last Tour de France we were to bring back an illus-
tration for this story of the bookshops in her provinces, and right
away in Valognes (petit Versailles du Cotentin), M. Loreuil and
his librairie 'Normannia' seemed the ideal subject. The English
idea too of the complete French bookseller with his three enthusiasms, *Les vieux livres, la pêche à la ligne, et la chasse.* He was
interested when I told him about this little survey of the bookshops of the provinces, most interested when I told him about the
Foreword, 'ah! comme ce monsieur Graham Greene écrit', but
when it came to his picture, Norman prudence started to nag,
with the '*P'têt ben qu'oui—P'têt ben qu'non*' which amuses and
annoys the rest of France. We were not going to get M. Loreuil's
picture but parted with the usual annual *grande amitié.*

We also parted with a more than usually interesting collection
of books from his shelves, the original edition of l'Abbé Hedelin's
classic *La Pratique du Théâtre,* 1657. A scarce Toulouse printing
(1671) of *Epigrammatum Joan. Oweni, Cambro Britanni Oxoniensis.*
A volume of anonymous eighteenth-century pamphlets including
Mémoire sur l'Electricité, 1746, with notices of earlier workers in
this field, Robert Boyle, Hawksbee, Gray, Nollet, etc. There was
one sixteenth-century work in the volume, the *Spiritalium Liber* of
Hero of Alexandria (Paris, 1583) with many beautiful woodcuts
of early chemical apparatus. For some Laurence Sterne collector,
there was a pretty little copy of *Nouveau Voyage sentimental,* Paris,
1784, bound with *Lettres d'Yorick à Eliza; augmentées de l'Eloge
d'Eliza,* par l'Abbé Raynal, Versailles, 1704.

For the collector of Americana, there was M. Campe's sequel
to what had been one of the best-selling children's books at the end
of the eighteenth century, his *Le nouveau Robinson.* This sequel
Découverte de l'Amérique, 1806, was in three small volumes beautifully illustrated. More serious Americana was *Le Conquérant de la
Californie,* a pamphlet by Alexandre Buchner printed in Caen in

1869. More light-hearted, and for our local vintner in Thame who collects early motoring books, was the *Album* issued by Panhard et Levassor in Paris in 1913, with beautiful coloured plates showing their drawing room Limousines and Landaulets (12.500 to 14.500 fr) also the dashing Torpedo (10 H.P., 4 cylinders, 9.300 fr).

We now hoped that the picture problem would be resolved by *une des vieilles dames bouquinistes* in Angers, but we had forgotten that one looked too scholarly to be asked to pose, and the other was too formidable. Then it all ended very happily in Perigueux where another old *bouquiniste* friend, Mme Christian de Sèze, at once entered into the spirit of the book, and was delighted with the idea of her picture alongside that of Mr. Ian Grant, chief of the clan of Scottish antiquarian booksellers.

With the *bon accord* between Scotland and France traditional since the sixteenth century, and still preserved in Aberdeen's alternative name 'Bon Accord', this juxtaposition seems doubly right.

Some American Customers

English customers want their books at economic prices from a sympathetic bookseller; American customers want a little more, and as they also want to give a little of themselves, one remembers them better. The first to be remembered was, however, neither English nor American.

The newspaper strike having put Lord Beaverbrook out of business, he appeared in Cecil Court one afternoon, and started to take down from the shelves any volumes whose binding took his fancy. Most of them were put back when he was told the price. As Chancellor of the University of New Brunswick he had been sending out to the university library so many books from his own library at Cherkley, that there were gaps on the shelves which he now wanted to fill. His idea of price was five shillings a volume for anything that looked handsome and learned. Even in those days it hardly seemed worthwhile, but the famous grin clinched a deal. When I phoned one day to say that there were a hundred or so volumes waiting to be collected, the reply was that his lordship was ill. Ten minutes later, a call from the *Daily Express* that his lordship would be most obliged if I would take the books down to Cherkley. The footman was worried about a load of books; the tradesmen's entrance was not mentioned, but as I seemed decided, he asked me to wait, returning rather a different footman with 'Would I please follow him up to his lordship's bedroom?' 'And the books?' I asked. 'I will get assistance.'

Lord Beaverbrook was in a large bed, with telephones on both sides. While the footman and I were lining up the books on the floor, he was taking and making telephone calls. When the books

had been nicely lined up in sizes, the telephones were cut off and
Lord Beaverbrook jumped out of bed to inspect, and for once
there was trouble. I think that he must have been bored with
no-one and nothing to harry, and he started to complain that this
and that was not worth five shillings. We then started to play a
little game on the nursery floor. There were now to be three lines,
five, four, and three shillings, with a few protests from both sides
to make it more exciting. The game ended, with Lord Beaverbrook, now quite happy, walking along the lines, stopping at one
heavily gilt morocco set and trying to read the long German title—
'Won't they think that I was a very learned person?' I didn't say
that there should have been three other volumes to complete the
set because after all, that was how I had been able to play games,
and make him happy. As he climbed back into bed he said 'It
must be fun being a bookseller?' and to my 'More fun than running a newspaper', the famous grin and 'I wonder?'

While the late E. P. Goldschmidt used to say that Americans
were his favourite customers because there was the Atlantic
between them, even he became involved in their infectious enthusiasm, although I doubt if our Donald Angus would have had
the success with E.P.G. that he has always had here. I met Donald
soon after he had come to Europe from Hawaii in the early
thirties, and decided that if America was his home, Europe,
England, and London were his true ambience. He made a great
collection on the South Seas and on Captain Cook which he has
now given to the University of Hawaii. At the beginning of the
last war, he was caught in the south of France, managed to get
back to England, and was an air-raid warden in London for a
short time before going back to America. He was back after the
war, but now with a villa in Tangier, less in London. Still, however, the postcards from Hong Kong, embassies in Athens or
Lisbon, or just from a boat somewhere in between. Three years
ago, a telephone call from nearby Waddesdon where he was
showing two old aunts the Rothschild mansion, 'Could he bring
them over to show them our roses?' Last Christmas I had written
Donald about a book on the pineapple, his second interest. It had

been written by William Griffin, gardener to John Manners, Esq., Kelham, Nottinghamshire, printed in Newark, 1808, a pretty little book in the original printed boards. 'Delighted, send it to Tangier', he wrote from Copenhagen, where he was spending the New Year, after Christmas in Amsterdam. He was just off to St. Moritz, but would I have lunch with him at the Ritz on his way back to Hawaii? On a cold January day, Oxfordshire looked more attractive.

Augustus Kelley of New York was a bookseller when I first met him after the war, and we went round the London and Home Counties' bookshops looking for our shared speciality. the economic and Radical history of the nineteenth century. A few years later, he became a publisher as well, and his current 162-page catalogue *Reprints: Economic and Allied Social Science Classics* is the best in this field of publishing, praised by authorities like Lord Robbins for the books selected, and for the editing by experts like John Saville of Hull University, and also for the reasonableness of the prices. In spite of his publishing commitments, Gus goes on calling here, unable to resist the oddment he has never seen before, and he has become a collector too. Last spring he flew over to join a trip round the great gardens of England, and while the party were in Oxford seeing Blenheim and the University Botanic Garden, he broke away for a couple of hours. He had become garden-minded while laying out his new Rhode Island garden. Conifers particularly fascinated him, and he went back to Oxford delighted with *The Yew Trees of Great Britain*, written by John Lowe in 1897. He asked me to try and find W. J. Bean's classic *Trees and Shrubs* in the three-volume edition of 1950–1. I have still not found a copy, so perhaps any other bookseller now reading these recollections and having a copy, will write and advise: Mr. Augustus M. Kelley, 305 Allwood Road, Clifton, N.J., U.S.A.

I will never know whether Andrew J. Onderdonk was a publisher, bookseller, or collector. I never sold him a book, but for eighteen months we had a most amiable correspondence. I think that he must have found my name in a bookseller's directory, because out of the blue came his first letter from Bad Ischl. He was having trouble with some slow payment from Oxford, maybe I could help? I replied that this would be rather delicate, but I could help with two of his other questions, 'Is the Bodleian the name of a man, or a geographical term?' and 'Is Oxford larger than Cambridge?' which I do know. To the last I added, 'Why not come and see, and have tea and muffins with us?' Muffins struck a chord, he had read about them in Thackeray, and once tasted them in a tea shop in Oxford Street, London, probably the old Buzzard's. He was an American, and had been in William James's class at Harvard, with the late T. S. Eliot as one of his classmates, but it was Henry James who was his hero. For heroine he had Peggy, a Bedlington terrier. During the winter of our correspondence, he wrote to Harrod's for a winter coat for Peggy. It was peacock blue trimmed with Persian lamb, and she was the smartest little thing in Bad Ischl. Congratulating them both, I told Andrew about the Sunday school class who were asked if they knew who Salome was, and a small boy said that she was the lady who danced in front of Harrod's. The correspondence ended as suddenly and mysteriously as it had begun. But Andrew J. Onderdonck was over 80, so it was probably quite natural, and I never wrote to ask why. I had just seen that haunting film *L'Année derniére à Marienbad*, and was grateful for this bookseller's version from Bad Ischl, with a supporting cast including William and Henry James, Cosima Wagner, and Peggy.

After the last war we had an order from Chicago for all the photographic items in the current catalogue. The order started 'Brothers' and was signed Alden Scott Boyer. As we had not sent him a catalogue, had never heard of him, and could find nothing out about him, we wrote that while the books were reserved for him, we would appreciate the reference normal with a first order. His reply started, 'Brothers, you've sure goofed this time', and included half-a-dozen references, with one from the Mayor of Chicago.

During the twenties, Mr. Boyer had thought up a Museum of American Household Antiquities. Apart from the old cameras, we only heard about the old sewing machines, and the bank building he had bought during the Depression to house the collection. For a few years we were appointed to help with old photographs and books on photography, then he tired of these, and wrote to the Eastman Kodak Museum in Rochester, New York, offering them the whole collection. The manner of the giving was pure Boyer. It was to be collected at the station on a certain day, but when the truck driver arrived he was told there was nothing for him, but a special train to the same consignee was waiting in the goods yard. The photography may have expired, but the correspondence, and Mr. Boyer's own photographs, went on. Photographs of himself, his home, the table specially laid for some anniversary of his happy married years with Mamie. The note-paper varied from the old flamboyance to the top of a packet of breakfast cereals headed 'Wrote from Joe's bar, 2 a.m.' Then one day a sober, sad letter saying that Mamie had died suddenly; he had bought a tent, and was going to camp on the shores of Lake Michigan along with dog Friday. He had seven dogs, each named after the days of the week, the other six he had given away, but he could not part with Friday. These were ex-performing dogs, and he drove them around with the boot of the car divided into little kennels. Mr. Graves, then manager of Brentano's Bookshop in Chicago, told me about the scenes in the shop when Mr. Boyer arrived with his troupe, some walking on their hind-legs and others *en-pirouette*. The sad little camp by the lake did not last long. Came a picture postcard from Great Rapids about his wedding. Very short this one: 'The service was beautiful, and the new car goes fine'. Later, I showed my most cheerful business file to the late C. K. Ogden, who thought that it should be preserved as a specimen, however untypical, of Anglo-American book relations in the twentieth century. He took it away saying that he would see it was deposited in the British Museum.

C. K. Ogden's interest in the Boyer correspondence established a link between the two men, poles apart in their careers. C. K. Ogden, famous as the Cambridge encyclopaedist, General Editor of the International Library of Psychology, the Sir Winston Churchill protégé, and inventor of Basic English. Alden Scott

Boyer the very wealthy American scent manufacturer. Both men were happy jackdaws who were not fussy about a little tinsel with their silver. The section may be headed 'Some American Customers', but by association, C. K. Ogden must follow Alden Scott Boyer, the further justification being that today all of Ogden's great library is at the University of California.

Although Ogden had been a customer before the war, it was not until some time after that I got to know him. He had called in one evening on his usual walk down from Bloomsbury to dine at the 'Athenaeum', and seeing a pile of books inside the door, asked what these were. I told him they were a new lot for the outside shelves. He had a good picking, and ever afterwards the query was, 'Anything new going outside tomorrow?' The new service was that his selections were taken downstairs till there was enough for a car load up to his house in Gordon Square, or to his bookstore in Montagu Street, W1. There were two other houses with books, in Brighton and in Buxton, but I never saw these. The two London houses were completely different. Montagu Street was so dingy that when we took our charlady along she told Mr. Ogden that working there would give her the creeps, however good the money. By comparison, Gordon Square, WC1, was sweetness and light, even with books everywhere. The staircase was shelved all the way up, and one evening, seeing four copies of Baron Corvo's *Chronicles of the House of Borgia* side by side, I asked why four? He said that having bought the first copy for a few pounds and liking it so much, he had to have the second when he saw it priced at a pound, and the other two followed on this good economic principle. In the large first-floor room his rare books shared with his collection of mechanical toys. The rarities were in bookcases and if there were piles of books all over the room, it wasn't chaos. Ogden had his reasons, this pile of seventeenth-century Shakespeariana for example, was work he was doing with a visiting professor from Illinois University. There wasn't a speck of dust anywhere, the glasses, decanter, and silver ashtrays gleamed. The house was run like clockwork by a couple who only saw the master when they brought his breakfast at noon, and a cup of tea when he left for his stroll towards the 'Athenaeum'. His working day was after the last guest had left sometimes well after midnight, with a less strenuous session in the afternoons. Dinner at the 'Athenaeum' was followed by his court in a corner of the smoking room with A. J. Munnings, C. S. Crawfurd, and Professor Bodkin as the regulars. There was an embarrassing dimming of lights and coughing by the porters before Ogden could be set off on his walk back to Bloomsbury. The last stages were very slow, because we had to stand at strategic corners of the Bloomsbury squares, while Ogden spoke through the dingy laurels to his alley cat friends. This was the difference between the two men, Alden Scott Boyer had his seven talented dogs, and C. K. Ogden an unknown number of nameless London moggies.

As for the great C. K. Ogden library, Dr. Lawrence Clark Powell, the librarian at the University of California who was responsible for its purchase, wrote in his fascinating *Books in My Baggage* (1960): 'It was like a transfusion of blood into a body. The nourishing effects of C. K. Ogden's collection will be felt forever throughout the University of California'.

When writing to give me permission to quote his assessment, Dr. Powell reminded me of the second great English library that he was instrumental in securing for the University of California: that of the late Right Honourable Isaac Foot, P.C. While there may have been many fewer books supplied from Cecil Court in the Isaac Foot collection, this too has its memories, less hilarious than those associated with C. K. Ogden's visits, but most soberly pleasant. In particular, there was Mr. Isaac Foot's last visit, when my partner, lately arrived into the firm, remembered a Commonwealth tract which he rather nervously showed to the great man who was delighted with it. To this day Billy Howard declares that it was this kindly appreciation that made him first feel that he was on the way to be a knowledgeable bookseller.

If Oliver Cromwell was Isaac Foot's hero, William Hazlitt was that of his son Michael when he first came to Cecil Court in his pre-parliamentary years. I never remember producing any sensational William Hazlitt find, but there were many Chartist and early Radical pamphlets helping to swell Michael Foot's well-known nineteenth-century Radical collection. I am not quite sure what sort of hero Isaac D'Israeli is to Michael Foot, but two years ago we sent him *Domestic Anecdotes of the French Nation* (1794), the anonymous and scarcest of all Isaac D'Israeli's publications. Acknowledging the arrival of this volume, Michael Foot added the kind of note that cheers on every bookseller: 'I was afraid that someone would have pounced before me. I have not seen a copy of the book anywhere else.' Would that more collectors came up with such generous unbuttoning!

Women Collectors

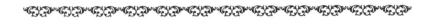

Most booksellers will say that there are no women collectors, so I am glad to remember the late Rose Macaulay on top of a ladder in Cecil Court, reading what she had pulled out of the shelves. She was curious about what other people collected and enjoyed hearing about bizarre collectors. When her flat in Luxborough House, Marylebone, was destroyed during the blitz, it was the loss of her library that grieved her most. She never had the heart to start collecting again, and became more and more faithful to the London Library.

Most booksellers will agree too, that even the most faithful of their customers weaken in the end, coming across a new face who at last completely understands their passion. I am glad to know that even after thirty-five years I have someone who goes on believing, and this not only an Australian but a woman too! Already in the thirties Mrs. Marjorie Grant of Melbourne had a good collection of early children's books, and she has been adding to it ever since. Maybe not in the Osborne class, but in the exhibitions which Mrs. Grant has put up all over Australia, her collection has been as culturally productive as the Osborne collection in Toronto. Early in our correspondence, Mrs. Grant had written about her baby Joanna, and once together with the order I included a book for the little Princess. The letters from now on were to give episodes in the life of the Princess, the first tooth, the going to boarding school, the engagement and the wedding group, the birth of James Hughes in July 1969, and, last Christmas, a picture of bouncing James and his ma.

For a further defence of women collectors, and of Australia.

From my current catalogue *Farming in Great Britain, 1600–1970*, I had a letter from a Miss Peel, also in the state of Victoria, saying that she had seen this catalogue in the university library and would like a number of the items in it. She included a cheque and the items she would like listed in order of preference till the cheque was exhausted. A state of virtue and modesty that one could never expect male collectors to understand.

At 94, Miss Ella Twynam is the oldest of my collector friends. Although she has given up collecting, she wrote, and I published for her two years ago a monograph on *John Toland, Freethinker, 1670–1722*. John Toland is her number one hero, followed by Voltaire, de la Mettrie, and Tom Paine. She has presented her Thomas Paine collection of books and pamphlets to the Paine Museum at Thetford, Norfolk, in memory of her old friend and collaborator Ambrose Barker. Now she is left with her Herbert Spencer books, which she must always have at hand. She was especially happy when two years ago I started a series of catalogues on the history of farming in Great Britain from 1600, because together with Radicalism, farming was the other tradition in which she had been brought up. These interests came from an adored grandfather who took charge of the little girl when her mother died young. John Talmadge Twynam had farmed at Whitchurch, Hampshire, during the eighteen-twenties and thirties, and has a niche in English farming history. In 1829, by crossing one of his Hampshire ewes with a Cotswold sire, he pioneered a new breed of sheep, the Oxford Down. A dedicated farmer, John Twynam was also an unusual farmer with Radical sympathies. In these, he was encouraged by the two great English radicals who also had farms in his home county. William Cobbett had once farmed at Botley, and John Twynam knew him and had many of his works. But it was Henry 'Orator' Hunt who was his hero. He had been at Hyde Abbey, a private academy for the sons of gentlemen in Winchester, with Henry Hunt's two sons. A few years later, Henry Hunt moved from Widdington Farm near Devizes, and bought Cold Henley Farm next the Twynam Whitchurch Farm. Young John Twynam was nearer his hero, though for most of the

time Henry Hunt was addressing meetings all over the country,
leaving his younger brother 'Dummy' to run the farm. Miss
Twynam has shown me her grandfather's diary where he describes
Henry Hunt's splendid physical appearance, and the great voice
which held his working-class audiences. There are notes on the
two most famous of these meetings, that at Spa Fields in 1817, and
in St. Peter's Fields, Manchester, two years later. About the latter,
John Twynam does not use either of the words 'Massacre' or
'Peterloo', which were to become the two most emotive words in
English Radical folk memory. John Twynam's diary also gives a
unique recording of the only known collaboration between the
two leaders, with William Cobbett coming down to persuade
Henry Hunt to give over a few of the fields at Cold Henley Farm
to the growing of his pet maize. Otherwise their very different
gifts kept them apart. William Cobbett, as shown in the definitive
M. L. Pearl bibliography, has 289 entries for published books,
pamphlets, and periodicals, and the *Dictionary of National Bio-
graphy* gives only three publications to Henry Hunt, but adding
that the whole of the English working class knew him as 'Orator
Hunt'. From the same diary comes a third and probably also
hitherto unrecorded anecdote on William Cobbett presiding at a
farmer's dinner at Odiham to honour the memory of Tom Paine.
Mr. Cobbett carved the large goose and found it very tough, so
he helped himself, then pushed the dish down the table with 'There
you are gentlemen'.

Keeping the diary, Miss Twynam gave me a pamphlet written
by her grandfather to put in my last catalogue. This pamphlet
To the Farmers of England generally, and of Hampshire particularly he
had printed in Andover, and published anonymously. He had
been amused at his little grand-daughter's interest in it, and for her
had pencilled his name in the margin: 'J. T. Twynam, Whitchurch
Farm, 1831 and 1832.' This signature, and Ella's confirmation,
were the only clue to the author, otherwise it would have been
only another of the nameless early English Radical pamphlets.
She was particularly happy when I told her how the Bodleian
Library had telephoned for this item, for it was now in the safest

of keeping, with the Oxford Down sheep not very far away. For my 'Radical collector' friends, and for my farmer friends who are not collectors, I would like to quote John Twynam's final paragraph in his Address: 'I appeal to my fellow farmers also to arrive at the conclusions, which have induced me, a farmer, and having staked my all in agriculture, to hail Reform, as the means of Salvation to my nigh-lost country.'

The Twynams are not yet finished with Orator Hunt. Miss Twynam still has her draft for a life, which she looks forward to seeing in print, although now busy with something she feels more urgent, the release of Rudolf Hess from Spandau. Her correspondence with the Foreign Secretary not having been very satisfactory, she is now going to write to Herr Willy Brandt. Last month I took over a German dictionary to Walthamstow, because she feels that it would be more polite to write in German—all this and more at 94!

Another two collectors were a long way off from Ella Twynam in her little Walthamstow flat with a home help, and meals on wheels. I was put in touch with the first by the Marquess of Cambridge, who was a director of Coutts & Co., Bankers, and used to call in at Cecil Court on his way to the Strand. As the Marquess only collected military prints and drawings, I never had very much for him, but one day I thought that I had, in a collection of Teck family books which a runner had brought in to me from the Caledonian Market. The Marquess was delighted, 'Wherever did you find that junk? We only chucked it out last week in a clear-up at home'. Some time later I showed him a pretty water-colour of the young Queen Victoria standing on the terrace at Windsor. 'You should let my aunt know about it', he advised, and I wrote to the Palace. Next day a trooper from the Household Cavalry came along on a bicycle to collect the drawing, and Queen Mary liked it.

A few years ago, a local sale turned up a folio manuscript diary kept by a James Anderson, gardener to Lord Kinnard, 1870–90, a fascinating eighteenth-century gardening chronicle, with details of plantings, and descriptions of the gardens at Glamis, and references to the Strathmore family. I wrote to Clarence House with a general description of the manuscript, and the reply, thanking me for bringing it to Her Majesty's notice, and would I please send it for her to see. A few days later, another letter from the lady-in-waiting: 'Queen Elizabeth finds it quite delightful and will be pleased to buy it'. With a further amiability, i.e., along with the cheque, came a note from the Clerk Comptroller: 'I wonder if you would be good enough to tell me who designed the heading to your notepaper? It has a most charming effect, and I suspect it must be Mr. Reynolds Stone', as it was.

Collections

Before the war, and before the London sale rooms became head-line news, the booksellers were able to buy private libraries, although I can only write about three.

The Margaret Barrie collection was composed of the books which Sir James had given to his favourite sister Maggie, and when she died around 1936 her son Willie Winter, British chess champion, and a friend, asked me to buy the books. It was a very special and personal evocation of Barrie and his author friends, with presentation copies from Conrad, Arnold Bennett, Gals-worthy, Hugh Walpole, and Leonard Merrick, but the only item I can still see is a splendidly wicked Max drawing at the front of *Fifty Caricatures*. Ten years earlier it would have been an exciting collection, but except for Joseph Conrad, the collectors of the mid-thirties were beginning to be uncertain about these names.

The Ambrose Barker books were as down to earth as the Barrie ones were 'fey'. The Barkers were a Northamptonshire family, and great Radicals. As a boy, Ambrose remembered his father intro-ducing him to James Watson, the last of the great Chartists, also taking him to support Charles Bradlaugh at the hustings in the election of October 1868.When Ambrose Barker came to London in 1878 as an assistant teacher at the Church Road Board School, Leyton, he at once joined the local branch of the National Secular Society. Two years later with the general feeling that the Society was concentrating too much on scientific secularism, rather than on a definite political creed, Ambrose led a breakaway from the local branch, founding the Stratford Dialectical and Radical Club. He was its first secretary, and from 1880 till his death in 1953, the

Club was in his bones. The History Workshop Pamphlet Number Five, *Club Life and Socialism in Mid-Victorian London*, by Stanley Shipley, shows the forty years of these working men's clubs up to the beginning of the First World War, as the most admirable phase in the history of socialism in England. The bitterness and strife of the first phase had gone, the political manoeuvrings had still to come. All his life, Ambrose Barker described himself as a revolutionary socialist; he had met Prince Kropotkin at a 'Russian Exiles' meeting in 1882, and took the chair when the Prince lectured to the Stratford club. With wages around thirty-six shillings a week, and a nine-hour day, membership of these clubs required enthusiasm, but that was always there. Science and poetry were equal parts of the lectures, with the top names of Edward Aveling, William Morris, Walter Crane, and Bernard Shaw. Further down the programme were spelling bees, brass bands, dances, and outings. While the Ambrose Barker collection was rich with Tom Paine, Robert Owen, William Cobbett, and the Chartists, it was the ephemera which he had collected as a background to these working men's clubs which made it unique.

If then the Barrie books were 'fey', and the Ambrose Barker ephemera 'earthy', the Pollitt collection was, as Oscar Wilde described Pollitt himself, 'gilt sunbeams masquerading in clothes'. Herbert Charles Pollitt was up at Trinity, Cambridge, in the early nineties. The most talked-about undergraduate, he was the central character in E. F. Benson's lightweight novel about the Cambridge of these days 'who possesses several of Mr. Aubrey Beardsley's illustrations from the Yellow Book, clustering round a large photograph of Botticelli's Primavera'. The undergraduate periodicals let themselves go on his theatrical performances, with the *Cambridge ABC* lyrical about his scarf dance, modelled on that of the American dancer Loie Fuller. As a memento of the sale of his books, I still have his Toulouse-Lautrec lithograph of Loie Fuller in that dance. From the E. F. Benson noting of the undergraduate interest in Aubrey Beardsley's work, Pollitt was to become the life-long champion and friend mentioned in Beardsley's last letter to his publisher, Leonard Smithers: 'Dear friend, I implore you to

destroy all copies of Lysystrata and bad drawings. Show this to
Pollitt and conjure him to do the same. By all that is holy all
obscene drawings, Aubrey Beardsley—in my death agony.'

I had been asked to come along and make an offer for the
Pollitt books just after the last war. In the main it was a marvellous
collection of the writers and artists of the nineties by a man who
had been friend and patron to many of them, and I did not feel
that I could value it adequately. Incidentally Pollitt always bought
three copies of his favourites. Two of these would have the bookplate designed for him by Beardsley, one of them he would read,
and the other keep mint. The third copy was to lend and give
away, as Pollitt was sure he would have to. Two years later, I was
asked to come along again, and this time instead of trying to make
out a price, there was an amiable arrangement by which I would
sell on commission, with no hurry on either side. Pollitt's heir was
happy, and I am sure that Pollitt would have been happy too.
Long before he died in 1944, he was looking back at the nineties
with a detached amusement. The way his books went, and the
friendships they founded, were just what he would have wanted.

Erotic Literature

Before the war, Erotica was a delicate, rather jolly perk for the self-respecting bookseller, having nothing at all in common with today's printing and reprinting of the graceless and non-human 'porn'. My favourite customer was a middle-aged fishmonger from Hull, who came down to London with his missis to see the shows twice a year. The first time he came into Cecil Court, I did have such a treat for him that he never forgot, and continued to believe that I was the bookseller of his prayers, but the timing was quite accidental. A widow had sent her husband's library to be sold at Hodgson's, and among the books was a box with a note asking for the books in it to be sold as discreetly as possible, if not destroyed. I was called in to help, and Hull appeared a few days later. I did not know the proper value of these improprieties, but Hull was delighted, although it was another two years before I was able to say 'Yes' to his cheery 'Owt for me lad?' Handing him the volume, he discovered that he had left his glasses at the hotel, so he and the missis sat down at the table in the front of the shop, where she read extracts and tried to describe some of the illustrations so that he could see whether the item measured up. Every bit as modest as her husband, she did have a finer appreciation of the setting, and when she lowered her voice he demanded 'Spake up lass!' I was glad that it was mid-morning, and that the shop was empty. Not everyone might have understood this homely little Yorkshire scene.

My most persistent customer came up from Whitehall at least once a week. He collected fine French bindings, but it was eighteenth-century French lewdicity in a contemporary binding and 'freely' illustrated that made his eyes gleam. He lived in Kent with a maiden sister who entertained the local curates, who did not entertain him. Not being in a hurry to get home, he spent the early part of the evening in the cosy little bar in Charing Cross station. There was no clash of loyalties between the parcel on the bar with its beauties after Moreau le Jeune and the stouter party behind the bar. My old friend was a bookman first, and he had been lucky with this volume which had arrived only that morning in Cecil Court. It had been sent along by a West End antique dealer who, when he was landed with books or a book, used to pass them on to me. When I went along to settle up, I thought that he looked exceptionally well, and said so. He said that he was just back from a week at Prinknash, and suggested that I tried a few days' quietness there. It was a Benedictine monastery in the woods above Gloucester, but that made no odds, it would be a harmonious change, and if I thought of a visit he would write to his friend the Abbot. I did spend a few days there, and when leaving the Abbot said that while they had been happy to have me there, they would have been happier if I had gone to one of their Offices. I went back in the autumn, and the following year was received into the Church.

That the most important personal recollection from these last forty years was appearing in the chapter starting with this fishmonger from Hull and ending with the Father Abbot of Prinknash, seemed mysterious to a cradle Scottish Presbyterian to whom John Knox should have made all things plain.

It was Metropolitan Anthony (Archbishop Anthony Bloom) who made the mystery plain. In his *Meditations on a Theme, A Spiritual Journey* (1972), he writes about these mysterious God-given chances, which are never to be questioned. They are just to be grasped, and to be continued to be grasped.

The Most Widely Known
Bookseller of our Time

I met Peter Kroger in Hodgson's sale rooms in 1955 as we were getting ready to leave London for Oxfordshire. When he heard where we were going, he said that as he lived in Ruislip, just off the London-Oxford Road, we must look in. We called one evening at the bungalow in Cranley Drive, and only got away by promising to come to lunch a week later. Lunch meant tea as well, and Helen insisting that she could find some supper too, even if, as on one occasion, there were eight of us to find for. The first time they came to lunch with us, Helen had to go into the kitchen and tell our housekeeper how much she had enjoyed her cooking. Our Mrs. Church was very touched, and hoped that we might have more nice people like these instead of the usual dry bookish ones. In the usual mumbled introduction, she had not grasped the name, and we never had the heart to tell her whom she had met.

Peter Kroger was a genuine book enthusiast, and it may have been this that shamed us professional booksellers into accepting a professional spy as a genuine bookseller. He even read the books he bought, and would come up with a volume, and a 'What do you think of this Dave?' He spent hours viewing the sales at Hodgson's, listing the titles in the composite bundles, and asking if he could stay on after the rooms were officially shut? Peter liked books, and they both liked people and fun. It seemed funny to us at the time, but it must have been funnier to Helen, when she told us how one day out shopping, she had parked the car at a 'no parking' sign. Told to move on, she had apologised and explained that she had just dropped her husband, Mr. Kroger. 'Glad to meet you, Mrs. Kroger' said the officer, 'I've had to show so many of your visitors the way to Cranley Drive.'

On the first Christmas after the trial, I sent Peter a card. His reply from Strangeways gaol, 'Number 5305, name Kroger . . . if such cards bring grains of happiness on the outside, they arouse mountains in here, mountains whose depths reach way down in one's being.' Maybe only a poet could have written *The Ballad of Reading Gaol*, but this for a *soi-disant* bookseller?

By Royal Appointment

'Wladislaus Quintus Dei Gratia Poloniae, Hungariae et Bohemiae Rex', or Count Potocki of Montalk, the rightful claimant, who, in 1936, made us by appointment (verbal), Booksellers to the Court of Poland.

The Count had walked into Cecil Court, with copies of *The Right Review* which he himself mostly wrote and printed. His get-up made sure of a subscription, a long purple robe, girdle, and chain *à la* His Beatitude Makarios, purple velvet beret with a large topaz in the front, and flowing hair. In 1936, this was Courage; in 1972 it would just have been another Sheep from the King's Road. As a person, he was as natural and surprising as his get-up. There were stories about the family's tribulations, mainly in New Zealand, with Uncle Bert, I remember, having had a particularly hard time, and it was all told in a gentle New Zealand accent. He, and pretty little Mademoiselle, and *The Right Review*, were to keep on drifting into Cecil Court until the war ended pleasantries.

Each Christmas we have a card from the Count, now settled with the Melissa Press in Draguignan (Var.). The last was a poem, *The Feast of Saturn and the Rebirth of the Sun*, by Count Potocki of Montalk, Villa Vigoni, Draguignan, with the printed time (of gestation?) 21 : x : 70—2.55–3.10 p.m. Along with the card was the prospectus of the Melissa Press, listing the seventeen of its publications available, also a generous advertisement for Richard Aldington's *Balls another Book for Suppression*, price five shillings. The prospectus also included Aldington's generous appreciation of the Count: 'All my congratulations. What matters is that your creative work should be available again. It is the only answer to the lavatory-seat wipers of literature who naturally don't recognise a poet and a gentlemen when by chance they meet him.' This prospectus 'priced at one shilling plus postage, unless we choose to give it away', and the seventeen works, can be obtained from the Melissa Press, Draguignan, Var., France. As Court Bookseller, let alone old pal, I would like to give this publicity to the Melissa Press, because of the difficulties which the Count experiences with other publishers in England. These he also described in the prospectus: 'They say that We are a difficult person to have dealings with. The truth is that We are an exceptionally good-natured, helpful, and courteous person. They imagine that We are a mere mutt, who can be put upon; and then they are indignant when this turns out to be incorrect.' I am happy indeed to have a patron who is not only royal, but polymathic too.

The Printer

The 1969 Winter number of *The Private Library* was given over to a long article on Guido Morris and the Latin Press, by Anthony Baker of the Bristol Reference Library, with an appreciation of the printer by F. G. B. Hutchings, President of the Library Association.

In 1966, Anthony Baker had been asked to make a catalogue of the library's holdings of works from private presses. Amongst these he came across the *Crescendo Series of Poets* printed and published by Guido Morris at his Latin Press in St. Ives, Cornwall, in 1952. The presswork was good, but this was the first that Anthony Baker had heard about it, and he set about making a note for a catalogue on the Latin Press, and that was the start of three years' writing, telephoning, and travelling about the country. First, no-one, supposedly in the know, could tell him anything about Guido or the Latin Press. *Penrose Annual, The Fleuron, Book Design and Production*, and *The Private Library*, all combed, but nothing. Then one clue took him to Hayward Marks, now in Coventry, but before the war a private printer in London. Hayward Marks suggested that he get in touch with the bookseller David Low, near Oxford. With my reply and reminiscences about Guido and his Latin Press, Anthony Baker was now under way.

In the summer of 1936, while staying in the Mendips, I was told about a young printer in the village of Langford whom I should go and see. Hick's Hay was a small whitewashed cottage. On the door was a beautifully printed broadside: *Guido Morris lives here with an army; the twenty-six soldiers of lead who can conquer the world and rout man's enemy.* Guido was a small semi-ethereal man, whom the villagers called 'the Grub', because he told them that he was grubbing for a living. The room one stepped into was a Printing Office, but the Columbia press, and some magnificent crimson curtains, are all I can remember. Guido lived, slept, and talked printing. He told me about the help and encouragement he was receiving from Mrs. Beatrice Warde of the Monotype Corporation, from Dr. John Johnson of the University Press, Oxford, and from Eric Gill. We became friends during that first visit because there was another contemporary hero whom Guido wanted to join up with, the late Gordon Craig. At that time, we were in touch with the great man, and Guido was fascinated to hear about those sometimes long and sometimes short, but always characteristic Craig letters. Before I left, I had promised to be the distributor for *Loquela Mirabilis*, a monthly periodical, which Guido meant to issue. During the next year, three numbers did appear from 17 Cecil Court, it was a very short year. Disaster came too in that year, with Guido suddenly coming in to Cecil Court to say that he was being sold up, and had come up to London for a general whip-round. We motored down to Bristol early next morning with the collection, and he managed to buy back the Columbia press and the type at the sale.

Guido and the Latin Press then moved up into the Mendips to a lonely cottage at the head of the Cheddar Gorge. I spent a week with them that autumn, Guido asking me to bring down my bed with me. When I arrived, the first thing was to run down to Wells to buy some food. It was splendid on top of the Mendips during a lovely autumn, but not so splendid when winter came. Guido and the Latin Press suddenly appeared in Redcliffe Road, Earls Court, where the main publication was Sir Basil Blackett's *Translations from the Greek*. Two years ago, I sent a copy to the Bristol Public Library, and Anthony Baker wrote that it was the best specimen of Latin Press printing that he had seen. From Redcliffe Road the press came across London down into the basement of the bookshop of my neighbour Peter Murray Hill. Peter was charmed to complete his establishment with a printer who would produce beautiful little editions of his theatrical ephemera.

The only production I remember was the broadside at the foot of the stairs: '*Tread carefully, this is Holy Ground, this is a Printing Office.*' The next misfortune, the war, was not Guido's fault and he did not believe it until the booksellers in Cecil Court started building up anti-blast walls of books in their windows. Guido now felt he should move again, and we suggested Cornwall.

A postman had left his bag at No. 17 and we filled it with bars of chocolate and biscuits for the hitch-hike down to Cornwall. I telephoned a sister, asking her if she would meet Guido and his girl at Ealing Common Underground station, and motor them as far west as she felt inclined. She spared them the suburbs, and set them on their way just beyond Maidenhead. It was to be two years before I heard what happened after Maidenhead. By then I was Bombardier Low in the Royal Artillery, and Guido, Private Morris in the Royal Army Medical Corps, and we met to have tea in the NAAFI canteen in Salisbury. There I heard how the first night out of Maidenhead, Guido and his girl slept under a haystack. The girl, waking early and probably thinking of these high heel shoes and the long way down to Cornwall, quietly slipped away. Guido waking, later and alone, gave up Cornwall and made for Northampton, where a sister had a café and a pretty waitress whom he married.

For a few months after the war, Guido was back in London seeing if bookselling was enough. It wasn't, so he finally got down to Cornwall and to the final flourishing of the Latin Press. And it *did* flourish at Carncrow, St. Ives, with the tentative checklist compiled by Philip Brown and Anthony Baker showing almost one hundred publications.

I had lost sight of Guido, until three years ago, when on the top of a No. 73 bus going down Shaftesbury Avenue, I saw him coming out of 'The Avenue' pub, in the L.T.B. uniform of a guard on the Underground railway. By the time we got to Piccadilly Circus I guessed that he was lost again. Anthony Baker ends *The Quest for Guido*: 'Some seven years from now (1969), Morris retires from London Transport, and then he hopes to "go to Paris until I die, or possibly Amsterdam, in which case I should hope to raise a small fortune and buy Enschedé types." "If that ever happens", reflects his old friend David Low, "how happy Paris or Amsterdam will be".' Earlier in his article, Anthony Baker quoted from another of my letters: 'This quest for Guido seems to be in the same genre as that for Corvo, though much much pleasanter', and there is another quotation from a letter to him from Sven Berlin: 'There is a touch of Corvo about him.' Superficial, and unfair of us both to Guido. For the Baron with the *gondolieri*, there was an uncomfortable, unheroic Death in Venice. There may not be much transport for Guido in the L.T.B., but there will be light at the end of the long, heroic tunnel.

With the final reckoning, as it should be, on Guido as Printer, I quote from F. G. B. Hutchings as he ends his article in the same Winter number: 'There is a greatness in Guido Morris, and his dedication to printing had the single-mindedness of the religious. In a monastery he could have made his gifts explicit to the world; in the world he was condemned to the conflict of trying to follow the light while his feet were caught in the contagion of ever-present necessity.'

St. Nicholas, old Joe's resting place

'Mons Rygnald de Malyns et due femes', 1385

Joe Malin, agricultural labourer, 1958

SOME EMMINGTON NOTABLES

Some
Emmington
friends

Emmington, Chinnor, Oxford

'Emmington, about 14 miles from Oxford, is a remote hamlet', and with the exception of our house built in 1938 this description in Methuen's *Guide to Oxfordshire*, 1906, could do for the hamlet today: seven cottages, two farms, the fourteenth-century church, rectory, and 'The Plough and Harrow'.

Chinnor is a village two miles south under the Chiltern Hills. Oxford, fifty years ago my university, is today our postal address. Oxford, proud of its libraries, and Chinnor unaware that its rectory once housed one of the most interesting of all English libraries, Sir Isaac Newton's.

When Sir Isaac Newton died intestate in 1727, an inventory of his effects was taken by order of the Prerogative Court of Canterbury. The inventory, discovered and described by Lt.-Col. R. de Villamil, showed that Newton left '372 books in Folio, 477 in Quarto, 1057 in Octavo, and Duodecimo, together with above one hundredweight of pamphlets and wast books'. They were in six book-cases and were 'valued at the sum of £270'. Four months after Newton's death, in July 1727, the library was bought by John Huggins, warden of the Fleet Prison. John Huggins, having also just bought the patronage of Chinnor, appointed his younger son Charles to the benefice, and sent the library down to Chinnor, where it remained until 1778. The Revd. Charles Huggins pasted his bookplate in each of the volumes, the Huggins arms, with beneath, 'Revd. Carol Huggins, Rector of Chinnor, in Com. Oxon'. Charles Huggins dying in 1750, a bachelor and intestate, his elder brother William appointed his friend Dr. James Musgrave to the benefice. Dr. Musgrave bought the Newton library from Charles Huggins's estate for £400, overpasting his own bookplate with the Musgrave arms and the motto 'Philosophemur'.

In the *Correspondence of Sir Isaac Newton and Professor Cotes*, edited by John Edleston in 1850, there is a note about the Swedish professor Bjornstohl making a special journey in 1775 from Oxford to Chinnor to see Newton's books, so they had not been completely lost sight of. But after Dr. Musgrave's death in 1778, they did disappear till Lt.-Col. de Villamil traced them down to Barnsley Park in 1928. Barnsley Park, just over the Oxfordshire–Gloucester county border, is the home of the Musgrave family, and it was here that they were taken by Dr. Musgrave's son and heir when he became the eighth baronet. When Lt.-Col. de Villamil discovered the Newton books once again, the number had sunk from the original 1,896 to 858. He was just a few years too late, in fact, to prevent the major loss from the Newton library. One of the Musgraves had married a Wykeham from Thame Park, a mile from Emmington. At the Thame Park sale in 1920, a number of the 'Philosophemur' books had been sent over from Barnsley Park to swell the books in the sale. The books were sold in bundles, with one of 200 volumes, and we had not yet arrived in Emmington.

This is the nearest Emmington has got to old books. To the inhabitants it is still a mystery how anyone can make a living in books without a bookshop. They kindly ask, 'Still writing books?' and now instead of mumbling, it is pleasant to be able to say 'Yes'.

If Emmington cannot produce an old book, it did at least have Old Joe Malin. Joe had been born, and lived all his life in the cottage across the road, and for 67 of his 78 years had worked on the same farm. When we published our first catalogue of books on farming in England from 1600 to 1970, Joe's picture was on the cover. He was a bit puzzled at the sub-title, 'The Last of the Normans', but that is what Joe was, at least in Emmington. A moat is all that remains of the original de Malyns house, though the famous fourteenth- and fifteenth-century brasses in the church of St. Andrew, Chinnor, still commemorate six of Joe's de Malyns ancestors. But all that Joe knew was that his father and grandfather had been shepherds in Emmington. Now, he was about the last of the English agricultural labourers. He had never been to London, thought Oxford 'a dirty old place', but before the war he had been taken on a village outing to Brighton, and Brighton was all that a town should be. When Joe spoke about 'the War', it seemed at first incredible that he was speaking about the English civil war, but in a strong, local folk memory, seven generations wouldn't let go of the only war in which Emmington had been involved. On 17 June 1643, Prince Rupert and his cavalry had ridden out from Oxford to burn out the Parliamentary headquarters in Chinnor. Coming back through Emmington, they blew up the Manor-House belonging to Richard Hampden, then turned to meet the pursuing Parliamentary force at Chalgrove. Joe was not interested in John Hampden, but he showed where Richard's house had once stood at the end of our garden, with its own gardens sweeping down to the Moat, now only a silted, reedy pond, hidden in willow and elm, but the joy of the wild duck who divide their time between our Moat and the lake at Thame Park.

Emmington can lift the mind wonderfully from too much contemplation of old books, and now for the first and last time, it has inspired a new one. If the background is books, the foreground is all people, and I would like to think of these tales as a translation, however homespun, of the International League of Antiquarian Booksellers' motto: *'Amor librorum nos unit.'*

WHERE'S ME?

An alphabetical guide to booksellers mentioned in the text